"A Toolbox of Tips!

...Life after graduation can be overwhelming and scary, and having this resource would have made my transition into the post-graduation phase much smoother."

—Amy Barth MSHR, Career Consultant and President, Transitional Futures

"This book is entertaining to read and presents the reader with practical ways to accomplish many of life's "chores"—whether 18 or 32 years of age."

—Christine Meyer, Executive Education Department, Duke University

"I wish *School's Out* was around when I graduated! O.Y. V.E.Y. (an Oblivious Youth who's constantly Vexed by Encumbering Yentas)."

—Steve Kriozere, writer/producer, *Spiderman* & *V.I.P.*

"An excellent instructional, practical, and amusing resource full of real life examples for graduates who want to make a smooth transition into the real world and succeed after school."

—Renata Slarova, Manager, Deloitte & Touche LLP

"Craig Hirsch's *School's Out* is a fun informative education for all students of life."

—Jordan Rush, writer/producer, *Coach*

School's Out

The Ultimate Cheat Sheet for Life After Graduation

Craig Hirsch, CPA

Window View Publications™
"Scouting Talent—One Book at a Time"™

www.WindowViewPublications.com
info@WindowViewPublications.com

ISBN: 0-9774544-0-1

This book is dedicated:

In loving memory of my father, **Dr. Marvin Hirsch**, who truly graduated with honors in everything he did.

&

In honor of my incredible wife, **Samantha**, whose love and support has accompanied me on every journey since kindergarten.

Table of Contents

Acknowledgments

"If you count all your assets, you always show a profit."

—Robert Quillen

Short, To-the-Point, But Very Necessary

Writing a book is no easy feat, especially on topics you have failed at before finally getting it right. It is for that reason that I am in a debt of gratitude to the many people who helped me succeed in understanding, digesting, and living the lessons and principles in the forthcoming pages. There are many people who have reviewed, edited, and offered constructive criticism on the manuscript, and for all their help, I am forever grateful. This mile long list includes all those who provided testimonials along with the following people who offered advice and constructive criticism:

Cover designer Elaine Lanmon, Brian Ross, Cliff Alsberg, Michael Chesal, Jonathan Seliger, Morris Rosenthal, editor Sharon Garner, Chuck Muhlbauer, Corinne Hirsch-Blumenstein, Barry Lynn, Carole Lynn, Heather Lynn, and of course, my charming and incredible wife, Samantha. Just remember fellas, Francois Duc de La Rochefoucauld said it best, "Gratitude is merely the secret hope of further favors."

Preface

"After eating an entire bull, a mountain lion felt so good that he started roaring. He kept it up until a hunter came along and shot him. The moral: When you're full of bull, keep your mouth shut."

—Will Rogers

Cheaters

Hank was just minding his own business—literally. Just getting comfortable in the airport bathroom, he suddenly heard a voice from the other stall. "Hi, how are you?" Hank wasn't the type to start a conversation in the restroom, but he didn't want to seem rude, so he answered, somewhat embarrassed, "Doing just fine!"

The mystery man in the other stall said, "So what are you up to?"

That got Hank thinking that this was just too bizarre. Unsure of how to respond, he blurted out, "Uhhh, I'm like you, just traveling!" Hank threw down the newspaper he had opened, and stood up, getting ready to leave the stall, when suddenly he heard another question.

"Can I come over?"

The blood rushed to Hank's face from embarrassment. He figured he would just respond politely and get out of the bathroom, so he replied, "No, I'm a little busy right now!"

As if on cue, the other person said, "Listen, I'll have to call you back. There's an idiot in the next stall who keeps answering all my questions!"

As Hank quickly learned, there are times in life when you feel awkward, confused, and helpless. You are asked questions and do your best to answer them, but in the end, you realize you've completely misunderstood the circumstance. Life presents many of those situations, especially when you're fresh out of school. Real life begins to unfold, and events arise that present doubt.

This book is the cheat sheet for real life. There are many aspects to life that nobody teaches you in school, and then—BOOM!—reality checks in with a rude wake-up call. This book is designed to help guide you through the realities of life without having to learn through trial and error. However, the chapters and lessons to follow are just like the cheat sheet—they will never take the place of the real McCoy. There will inevitably be particulars and aspects to topics that you will learn when you face the real world. But, as you probably know, using a cheat sheet can often be a life saver.

When I was in college, I soaked up every academic course I could. Once I graduated, I realized I didn't know anything about real life. For starters, filling out the W4 form on the first day of work was torturous. I had to use a magnifying glass just to decipher the words. Then there was the time that my girlfriend—now wife—asked if we could make dinner together, and the only thing I could readily identify was the start button on the microwave. But, positively, the most agonizing aspect to growing up was the fact that my mom paid thousands of dollars in tuition, and my tighty-whities were still coming out pink.

But I learned the hard way, as most do, after school. I ventured into the real world, and discovered, by trial and error, all the knowledge in the pages to follow. There have been countless books, articles, and seminars offered on each of the topics discussed. It would have been easy to write an entire series on one of these topics alone! The purpose is not to make you a world-renowned expert in any of these areas. Rather, it is to give you something most graduates don't have: a heads-up on real life. It's a taste of what's out there and it teaches you the lingo and concepts before you get clobbered.

This book is not laced with fluff. It's the cheat sheet of real life, containing the essential teachings of how to weave your way through the sometimes heavy traffic of reality. When school is finally out for the last time, you might be afraid or intimidated about some of the new experiences you will soon encounter. But, unlike your predecessors, you'll have a jump-start on reality by reading through the pages ahead. Read it, digest it, and then undertake the most daunting task of all—live it. The following lessons will help guide you through the challenges of life after school, and if you learn from Hank and observe your surroundings, you'll never be caught with your pants down.

CHAPTER 1—PEOPLE, RELATIONSHIPS, & WORK:
The People's Court

"In prosperity, our friends know us; in adversity, we know our friends."

—John Churton Collins

Up Close and Personal

Unless you're a hermit and plan on hibernating inside a dark cave for the rest of your life, odds are that you will be interacting with people. Making first impressions in social circles, knowing what to say and how to say it, and interacting with business associates are all essential skills. Some are born with a natural ability to schmooze, while others have trouble relating to anything that's not a number. Even if you're proud of the disgusting habits you mastered as a teenager (like when you threw a party when your burp was louder than the Richter scale could handle), you might want to pretend that wolves didn't raise you.

In this chapter, you will learn how to:

- Make a dynamic and memorable first impression

- Get through to the busy people who have been evading you

- Prepare an eye-catching and impressive resume

- Interview with poise and professionalism

- Negotiate effectively

I. First Impressions

Face-to-Face for the First Time

You may have heard the common phrase, "You don't get a second chance to make a first impression." This is one of the most accurate clichés around. It might be wrong, upsetting, and simply unfair, but the reality is that people are judgmental and form an opinion in the first few seconds of meeting you. Every person has multiple layers of personalities, and some are shy at first while others are outgoing. Some are friendly, some are vicious (think the Big Bad Wolf). Regardless of your personality, there are universal tips that everyone can use to make a positive first impression.

The Most Important Thing

While there are many things you should keep in mind when making a first impression, there is one item in particular that stands out from the rest. This component is so critical, it will forever leave an imprint on any poor victim who has the unfortunate luck of meeting you for the first time. The very first thing you need to do is check for any loose or hanging B.O.O.G.E.R.S.:

Be Interested—Most people like to talk about things that have meaning to them. Their annoying toe callus and favorite pooper-scoopers might not be the most interesting topics, but if it has meaning to them, it has meaning to you.

Open your ears—This is the most important factor of all. When you are interested—and, yes, that means you have to try to genuinely make an effort—you have to listen courteously. Your doing so will make the other person appreciate your consideration. It might sound trivial, but don't downplay it. Part of human nature is a big ego, so if you want to make a good impression, stroke their ego by listening attentively.

Oops! I was mistaken—It is simply not a good idea to get into an argument with someone you just met for the first time. Even if you're right—and often you will be—suck it up, and simply say, "I could be mistaken." Although you're passionate about the protein you get from chocolate-covered grasshoppers, to the other party, they will recognize that you are an agreeable and pleasant person, one with whom they will want to associate further if you concede.

G*room yourself*—This might sound ridiculous, but the way you look is important. Appearing as if you just jumped out of bed, with hair that looks like you stuck your finger in an electrical socket is not the way to get off to a good start. Brush your teeth and hair, and make sure you don't have any leftovers from lunch dribbling down your sleeve. Being presentable might not make you memorable, but portraying yourself as a slob will make you unforgettable.

E*ye Contact*—Try something like, "You have beautiful eyes, my dear." You don't have to get as dramatic as the wolf from *Little Red Riding Hood*, but eye contact is crucial. There's nothing worse than talking to someone while you are busy looking over their shoulder for another friend. When you are involved in a discussion with someone, maintain eye contact and show that your full attention is on them.

R*emember their name*—Yup, it's about name-calling here. Believe it or not, by using the other person's name in your conversation, it will add the extra personal touch. They will be impressed that you cared enough to remember their name. So, even if it is seventeen syllables in length and you need a dictionary to help you pronounce it, make the effort to use it throughout the conversation.

S*mile*—Even if you only have one front tooth. That's the attitude you need when meeting people for the first time. Studies prove that those who smile and seem happy are likely to attract the most friends. That's because their positive demeanor and upbeat personality make them someone everyone wants to be around. Force yourself to smile—even if you're having a bad day—and, who knows, the day might take a drastic U-turn. (If you really do only have one front tooth, you might want to see a dentist).

Getting Through to Busy People

It's quite difficult to get through to people who are very busy or important. Very often, you'll get their assistant, who will say, "The Big Dog is way too busy to speak with you, so let me patch you through to his voice mail." This can be frustrating, discouraging, and time-consuming. You've heard all the tricks about how to bypass the secretary, but most of them are based on lies and fraudulent behavior (like the one where you distract the secretary with beautiful roses, then plunge into the corner office unannounced). Here are some ethical tricks of the trade to help you to speak to the Big Dog (in this example, Ms. Mona Lott) faster:

1. If you find yourself leaving too many messages, without the person returning your call, simply say, "Hey, Mona. I'll be in your area and I'm planning to drop by." You'll be amazed at how *few* people want you "dropping by."

2. If you've never met the person before and they are not responding to you, leave a cryptic message as if you know them, sparking their curiosity as to who you are. Leave a direct message, saying, "Hey Mona. Amanda Huggenkiss here in South Florida. Gimme a call back when you can. Number is 555-222-3333." When people hear a message that sounds as if you know them, they will be itching with curiosity to know who you are and will call back promptly.

3. If you reach the executive assistant one too many times, don't ask the typical question, "Is Mona Lott available, please?" Rather, you should be assertive and phrase it in a statement, such as, "This is Denise R. Nockin calling for Ms. Mona Lott." Believe it or not, this sounds like you're an important person who is fitting Mona into *your* hectic schedule. Chances are, the secretary will either put you through to Mona or get your message to her sooner than other waiting messages.

II. Preparing Your Resume: It's E.A.S.Y.

The Purpose of the Resume

Many people have the mistaken impression that a great resume gets you a great job. The truth, however, is that a great resume will get you an interview. The interview is all about presentation and your social skills. But you won't get the interview without a great resume.

It's E.A.S.Y.

Preparing your resume can be summed up in one word: easy. Once you know what job you're applying for and have done sufficient research, writing your resume can actually be fun. Assuming you have your goals and objectives clear, it should be *easy* to write it. It should be *easy* to get the interview after your resume is read. But more importantly, your resume should be *easy* to read. Get the drift? Good, go take it E.A.S.Y.:

Everything You've Ever Done

Apply It to Your Desired Job

Simplify the Resume

Yearn to Make It the Best It Can Be

Step #1: **E**verything You've Ever Done

The Golden Rule

Don't lie. It's unethical and simply not worth it. References will be checked, backgrounds will be investigated, and, eventually, the truth will unfold. So, as you begin your journey in building your resume, just remember: lying simply doesn't work. Besides, who is honestly going to believe that you worked for the FBI, produced four hit television shows, and acted as the President's speechwriter—all as an intern during the summer?

Make a Laundry List

The first step of the resume is to write an exhaustive list of everything about you. Education, work experience, hobbies, extracurricular activities, awards, and anything else you can think of. This list will help you organize your thoughts in the second step, when you are applying it to your coveted job objective. So write down everything about yourself (okay, you don't have to write down the itchy rash on your thigh) into a nice long list.

Education

If you're straight out of school, your education is probably the first thing most people will glance at. You don't need to have attended Yale in order to attract attention, but be aware that it is important. If you're graduating college, list only the colleges you attended, leaving out any high schools. And, if you are graduating high school, leave off those kindergarten years, as memorable as they may be.

Work Experience

Nobody expects your work experience to include the Pentagon, Chief Financial Officer of a new public company, or NASA, but potential employers do want to see where you've worked. Even if it was for short periods of time (e.g. after school, weekends, summers, etc.), write them down on your list. Remember, you can edit this later. But, for now, write down all jobs you've held (except for that taste-testing job that you got fired from for eating the boss's lunch).

Extracurricular Activities

Do you volunteer to feed the homeless? Are you on a sports team? Do you specialize in fake IDs? Whatever your interests (with the exception of the last example), write them down. Just make sure they're legal, and you won't run into a problem.

Step #2: Apply It to Your Desired Job

The Objective

The objective is a one-line heading on the top of a resume that is just that: it states your desired goal. An example of an objective is: "To obtain a position in the field of milking cows." Some professional recruiters hate them, others love them. Their purpose is to show that you've got a direction and goal as to what you want out of the job.

Include the objective, as it shows that you have determined where you want to direct your career.

Highlight Areas of Relevance

Now comes the hard part. With your jumbo list of everything you've ever done, you need to sift through it and determine which work experience is your biggest weapon. This should be the experience that you can brag about. Most likely, this will be the work experience you want to focus on. However, there are two main categories of resumes.

Types of Resumes: Chronological and Functional

There are many types of resumes, but the two most common are the chronological resume and the functional resume. The chronological resume goes in timeline order, from most recent all the way back to your first job. This is the most common one used and, if you're coming straight out of school, use this one. The functional resume focuses on *what* you did, not when and where you did it. It is grouped by skills and qualifications and is usually used when your work experience does not match your career goals and aspirations. For example, if your most recent experience was a garbage-can gofer, and you are applying for a job as a shark keeper, you might want to use a functional resume, and list your childhood experience of caring for your pet goldfish first, as that experience closely relates to a shark keeper (and then place your trashy gofer experience below it). But, for most students coming out of school, the chronological resume is the best fit.

What to Write

On the chronological resume, you should aim to have two or three jobs posted on your resume. For each job listing, you will need to write the name of the company, job title, time you were there (e.g. Summer 2006), the city and state where the company is located, and several bullet points as to what you did there. See the example resume below which emphasizes where to place all these items.

References

At the very bottom of your resume, it is a commonly accepted practice to write "References Available Upon Request." You'd like to stop there, but this means that you actually have to prepare a listing of references. On a separate sheet of paper, write down five names, plus the company name, title, address, phone number, fax number, and e-mail address, of people who will say really nice things about you. It is also advisable to list your relationship with them (e.g. employer, religious leader, drug dealer, etc.) beneath their contact information. These people can be your former employers, teachers, or religious leaders. But if there is someone who would rather see you rot in a place that's very hot, you might want to save them for another list.

Step #3: Simplify the Resume

Solution Oriented

In each of the bullet points of your work experience, list all your responsibilities. With most summer internships, you probably manned the phones and faxes, sent off Fed-Ex packages, and other similar tasks. Potential employers will already know this is what you've done. So, to make yourself stand out just a little, focus on detailed items and specific problems that you helped solve. For example, if you fixed the plumbing when your job was only to clean the sinks, you can say you went above and beyond the call of "duty."

Convert All Activities Into Crowning Accomplishments

It makes an enormous difference in the resume if you convert each activity you performed into an accomplishment. Structure these sentences by starting off with an action word (see the list below), followed by the activity, and what you accomplished. Heed the golden rule, however, and refrain from lying. With this exercise, it's easy to get carried away and exaggerate the truth. For example, if you licked 600 envelopes instead of using a glue stick, it is probably misleading to say that you "Reduced operating expenses by 25 percent by improving efficiency and eliminating excess office supplies." Don't exaggerate or lie. Just tell the truth in a way that makes you look good, demonstrates that you accomplished a worthwhile task, and shows that your tongue hasn't lost all of its taste buds.

An Example

As an example, if you interned at an insurance agency and helped an agent organize a sales seminar, you could write, "Coordinated 401K sales presentation, launching a 10% increase in sales from previous years." The way to emphasize this is by using action words and specific details. Quantify the results by including numbers and statistics, which are usually very easy to calculate. These words articulate what you've done and make your work experience sound more professional. Consider using the list of action words listed below when developing your bullet points.

Action Words

- achieved
- acquired
- adapted
- addressed
- administered
- analyzed
- anticipated
- assembled
- assisted
- audited
- budgeted
- calculated
- centralized
- changed
- collaborated
- composed
- condensed
- conducted
- constructed
- contracted
- converted
- coordinated
- created
- cultivated
- demonstrated
- designed
- developed
- devised
- discovered
- doubled
- drafted
- edited
- eliminated
- enforced
- established
- evaluated
- expanded
- explained
- forecasted
- formed
- founded
- generated
- guided
- hired
- implemented
- improved
- informed
- insured
- interpreted
- interviewed
- launched
- maintained
- managed
- marketed
- maximized
- minimized
- motivated
- negotiated
- obtained
- operated
- organized
- originated
- oversaw
- performed
- planned
- prevented
- produced
- programmed
- promoted
- provided
- publicized
- published
- recruited
- reorganized
- reported
- researched
- resolved
- reviewed
- selected
- separated
- set up
- simplified
- solved
- surveyed
- staffed
- supervised
- taught
- tested
- trained
- used

White Is Right

Some are under the impression that they have to write elaborate essays on what they've done at their job. The potential employer would almost always disagree. Recruiters want to see a one-page resume (two pages are acceptable, but that's only if you've been around a long time, and unless you failed second grade ten times, you won't fit that category). On this one page, they want to see short, concise sentences describing your qualifications and experience. So, if you see space on your page that's white, you're probably in the right.

Step #4: Yearn to Make It the Best It Can Be

Spell Check and Grammar Check

Once you think you're finished and the resume is complete, it's time to put it through the review process. The first step is to do a spelling and grammar check. Remember, this is one piece of paper, but it's pretty important. So go through it with a fine-tooth comb (brushes don't work as well), and make sure it's ready to be seen by the outside world.

Consistent Layout

Make sure that you use the same font throughout, and that all headings look the same. You don't want similar parts to be bold and underlined, while others are missing the bold feature. Be sure that if you used bullet points on one job, you are not using number form on the next one.

Ask for Feedback

Never send out a resume before asking someone to glance over it. You can make natural mistakes that may only be caught by someone looking at it with a fresh eye. Besides looking for obvious mistakes like grammar and misuse of words, independent third parties may be able to offer advice about other items to include or certain parts that should be taken out. Be sure to show it to friends, family members, and colleagues, as they can help put the final touches on it.

Bill Loney

123 Desperate Lane, #106   555-123-2064
Slaughter, KY 12345   BiLoney@milker.com

OBJECTIVE: To secure a full-time position in the field of milking cows.

EDUCATION: Slimy University, Mud Lick, KY
               B.S. in Professional Farming, Cum Laude, May 2010
               Overall G.P.A.: 3.68; Major G.P.A.: 3.84
               Honors: Dean's List 2008-2009

RELEVANT COURSEWORK: Principles of Milking, Intermediate Planting, Advanced Organization of Livestock.

WORK EXPERIENCE:

Uncle Buck's Dairy Farm, Inc.   Friendship, TX
Assistant to Lead Farmer   **Summer 2009**
- Designed "Squeeze and Hold" udder technique, increasing production two-fold
- Promoted milk with interactive campaign, tripling sales from the previous year
- Assisted farmers in rearing cattle, often over 40 animals at a time
- Trained geese to behave, honking politely when feeding time arrived

Gardening International, LLC   Cut Shin, KY
Researcher   **Summer 2008**
- Developed critical components of the Corn Cutter revolutionary product
- Recommended improvements for picking tomatoes without using hands
- Analyzed key body oils that contribute to food contamination
- Promoted the "Mud Is Fun" campaign, boosting sales by 65% in three months

EXTRACURRICULAR ACTIVITIES:
Author, *How to Milk Three Cows With Two Hands*   Fall 2008
Founder, *Farmer Scouts*   Summer 2007
Member, *Slaughterhouse Association*   Fall 2005—Summer 2006

SAMPLE COVER LETTER

Bill Loney
123 Desperate Lane, #106
Slaughter, KY 12345
(555) 123–2064
BiLoney@milker.com

January 1, 2010

Mr. Brock Lee
Farmer John's, Inc.
Udder Grabbing Lane
Grow, TX 54321

Dear Mr. Lee:

Recently, I completed a cooperative experience with a professional farming company in Friendship, Texas, where I was given the responsibility of assisting cow-milking professionals. I am looking for the opportunity to expand my responsibilities and perform as a professional farmer at Farmer John's, Inc. I believe my background and experience will be an asset to your company in a very short time.

I have conducted survey and mapping assignments, have participated in soil exercises, and have performed in goat-herding tournaments. I have also received nominations and awards for expertise in milking, slaughtering, and planting, all while within the legal parameters and ethics of the profession. My communication skills are excellent and I am conscientious about meeting expectations and completing unsupervised tasks. If given the opportunity to milk one of your cows, I will prove that I meet the needs of your company.

Further, I am very interested in becoming a part of your farming family after reading your company brochure. I became interested in your company after reading an article in *Farmer's Journal* about your company's reputation for outstanding sharecroppers. I can be reached at the address and phone number above. I'll be calling your office within ten days to inquire about the status of my application. I look forward to hearing from you.

Sincerely,

Bill Loney

SAMPLE THANK YOU LETTER

Mr. Brock Lee
Farmer John's, Inc.
Udder Grabbing Lane
Grow, TX 54321

Dear Mr. Lee:

Thank you for taking the time to meet with me regarding the cow-milking position at Farmer John's, Inc. After meeting with you and observing the company's operations, I am confident that my background and skills correspond with your needs.

I really appreciate that you took so much time to acquaint me with the company. It is no wonder that Farmer John's is the premier farm where all cows want to be milked. I am convinced I could learn a great deal from you and would enjoy working with your stellar staff of professional farmers.

I also value your advice for improvement, including refining my ability to milk cows without injuring their udders, rearing cattle, and gathering geese in an orderly fashion. I also enjoyed learning that the French word for farmer is *boer*.

I look forward, Mr. Lee, to hearing from you concerning your hiring decision. Again, thank you for your advice, time, and consideration.

Sincerely,

Bill Loney

III. Interviewing Skills

You're Hired!
The two words everyone wants to hear after they've come back from an interview. While most students think this section only relates to the business world, you might be shocked to learn that interview skills will help you in many other situations. There are many circumstances that require you to go through the interview process—such as getting into college, country clubs and condo associations, adopting your pet giraffe, and, of course, the work force.

What It Takes
Interviews can be stressful, time-consuming, and, in some cases, discouraging. Successful interviews stem from a myriad of things, such as confidence, intense preparation, research, social skills, and luck. As far as the luck factor goes, it's usually out of your control. Such examples of luck can include whether the company is strapped for more resources or if the interviewer is having a good day. (If you were the recruiter and everyone noticed your fly was unzipped, would *you* want to employ more people to make fun of you?)

Before the Interview
This is where it all starts. And, with interviews, starting off on the right foot is of key importance. Here are some tips when preparing for your interview.

1. Resume—This is the cornerstone of the interview. The interviewer will usually look over your resume prior to your interview, so they will likely ask you questions based on what you put on your resume. When designing your most precious document, ask advice from parents, friends, and counselors. A good resume will be only one page, with the necessary and impressive information in clear and easy-to-read bullet points. Don't rush this part of the process, as it is crucial that it be done correctly.

2. Letter of Recommendation—While not as important as the resume itself, it is impressive if you have one or two letters of recommendation from former employers, teachers, or religious leaders (remember, a drug dealer isn't the most

reliable source).

3. Research the Organization/Company—Remember what was mentioned about first impressions: you always want to make the other person feel important. It's no different in an interview. Research the company or organization that you are interviewing with, and be sure to ask at least two to three questions on specific topics and current events the organization is encountering. Have these in your mental arsenal, ready to be fired away during the interview. One of the biggest turnoffs to an interviewer is when the candidate knows little about their company. Research them, stroke their ego, and brag about how much you've learned about their company (no need to mention the lawsuit where one of the employees is suing them for getting fat off of their Friday doughnuts).

4. Practice, Practice, Practice—Grab a friend and get a list of the most commonly asked interview questions (from countless Web sites, magazines, journals, and books). Then go through multiple interview rounds, having your friend ask you many of the questions. This mock interview will give you a sense for the real thing. And, who knows, some of the practice questions may even come up in the actual interview itself. Here are some of the most common questions an interviewer will ask:

    a. Why did you decide to enter this profession?
    b. What are your strengths and weaknesses?
    c. List a few of your most important/proudest accomplishments.
    d. How do you work in groups, and what experience have you had working in groups?
    e. What appeals to you about this position?
    f. What would you say you learned from your college/graduate school experiences that you see being carried over to your life today?
    g. Describe a problem person you have had to deal with. What did you say or do?
    h. What important goals have you set in the past, and

how successful have you been in working toward their accomplishment?

   i.   What motivates you to put forth your best effort?

   j.   What do you see yourself doing five or ten years from now?

5. Dress For Success—Physical appearance for both men and women definitely counts, so, in addition to brushing your hair, teeth, and anything else that smells or looks funny, you should also wear formal business attire. Unless told otherwise, wearing formal clothing is the commonly accepted dress code for an interview. Even if you are overdressed in isolated circumstances, the interviewer will be impressed with your respect and value for their organization.

6. Confidence—Before walking into the interview, make sure you believe in yourself. While there are other candidates for the job, believe that you are the best qualified. Just as your DNA is unique, so are your personality and skills. If you don't believe in yourself, nobody else will. As an old friend once said, "Success comes in cans, not cant's."

During the Interview

Okay, this is it. You've spent a long time preparing and researching for this interview. Here are the most essential things to remember when heading into the "chamber of doom." Follow the rules, and you'll be pleased to hear you're H.I.R.E.D:

Handshake—It's game time. Your handshake is like the opening kickoff on Super Bowl Sunday. Extend your hand, give a firm grip and pump it twice. Squeeze too hard and your interviewer will call security. Offer him a limp hand, and he'll think you need a blood transfusion. Hold his hand too long, and he'll think you want something more than a job. Just shake hands professionally.

Initial Contact—On the first encounter with the interviewer, offer a firm handshake (see above), smile, and immediately introduce yourself. It always adds flavor when you sincerely say that you've been looking forward to meeting the interviewer and that you are excited about having the opportunity to come in for an interview.

Remove Your Cell Phone!—It seems obvious, but you'd be surprised how many people forget. If you need to keep it on in case of an emergency, be sure to turn the mode to "vibrate," and should the instance arise where you must answer it, explain to the interviewer in a calm, professional manner, that you have a personal emergency that needs immediate attention.

Engaging Body Language—When you enter the interviewer's office, there will often be multiple chairs for guests. Be sure to take the one closest to the interviewer, as it shows you are eager to be close to them. Just don't get freaky on them and ask to sit on their lap. Polite posture is of key importance. Folded arms or a slouching position indicate a lack of enthusiasm and interest. Sit straight, be relaxed, confident, and friendly, and your demeanor will instantly score you some brownie points.

Don't Forget to Ask Questions—Usually, toward the end of the interview, you will be asked if you have any questions. This is where your preparation truly pays off. You should take the opportunity to impress your interviewer with the knowledge you've accumulated about their organization. Don't overwhelm them with useless questions, such as what they serve for lunch, and if their urinals are built high enough for your tall body. Just be informative and to the point. Ask two to three questions that show you've done your homework. For example, at the end of your interview at McBurger Queen, it would be appropriate to say, "I've read that sales have tripled since the price of the McQueen Triple Burger was reduced to 99 cents. How has that affected your company?" Although everyone wants to ask it, the one question you shouldn't ask on the first interview is: "You're planning on paying me the big bucks, right?"

After the Interview

Whew, now it's over. You've shaken the interviewer's hand for the last time (for your sake, make sure there is no sweat on yours). You might think this process is over, but the reality is that there is more work to do.

1. Send a Thank-You Note—This is the final touch that shouldn't

be forgotten. Don't underestimate the power of a well-written thank-you note. Be sure to highlight some of the topics discussed in the interview. Thank your interviewers for the chance to meet with them, and that you look forward to hearing from them soon.

2. The Second Round—Some companies have multiple rounds of interviews, so if they call you back and ask you to come in for a second or third round, that's a good thing. Just be on your toes, because they are narrowing the competition with each round!

3. Follow Up—It may take the interviewer some time to get back to you. They may have to discuss their hiring need with their managers, owners, or partners in the company. The appropriate time period to wait is about 2-3 weeks after the interview before following up. At that point, it is perfectly acceptable to send the interviewer a follow-up letter. Mention that you are curious about your status and when you might expect to hear from them. Although some have tried it, don't threaten the company by picketing naked outside their office until you receive a response.

Web Sites to Look For Job Openings

www.hotjobs.com
www.craigslist.com
www.careerjournal.com
www.monster.com
www.careerbuilder.com
www.ajb.com
www.dice.com
www.resume.com
www.jobweb.com
www.employmentguide.com

IV. The Negotiator

Life Isn't Fair

Sooner or later, you will realize that you can't always get what you want in life. But there's nothing stopping you from trying. Knowing how to negotiate with car salesmen, apartment landlords, and the kidnapper who is threatening to slaughter your pet hippopotamus can save you a lot of money. Negotiating is not easy, but when done correctly, it can be really rewarding, not to mention fun.

The Ground Rules

There are hundreds of negotiating rules, but here is the list narrowed down to the top ten. These are the must-have ground rules if you want to have a fighting chance as a negotiator. If you follow them properly, you will be a negotiating P.O.W.E.R.H.O.U.S.E.

Prepare Properly

Only Talk With Authority

Who Needs It the Most?

Emotions Are Unacceptable

Respect Your Rival

Honest Facts Only!

Offer Your Rival a Winning Solution

Understand the Other Party

Sacrifice Without Slaughtering—Compromising

Equipped to Walk Away

Rule #1: **P**repare Properly

This is the first, and probably the most important rule. Being prepared has many factors, including knowing your main objective, learning everything you possibly can about your rival, anticipating where arguments will arise, solutions you will propose, and deciding what you are willing to compromise. Preparing properly means doing a "mental dress rehearsal" of the actual negotiating.

Rule #2: **O**nly Talk With Authority

Often you will argue with someone for long periods of time, making sound arguments and superficial headway, only to discover that the person you have been arguing with has no authority to give you what you want. So, before you whip out your notepad or spew out your arguments and logic, make sure the person listening can actually do something about it.

Rule #3: **W**ho Needs It the Most?

If your challenger is the one who needs the deal more— congratulations! You have a large amount of leveraging you can do. However, if you need this deal more than your rival, you'll need plenty of preparation beforehand. You will need to anticipate what will make your rival happy, and what you can afford to compromise. However, if you are the one who needs the deal more, be careful not to show it in your facial expression. Odds are, your rival will try to take advantage of you. If you remain firm in your stance and physical demeanor, you'll have a better chance of walking away with a win-win situation.

Rule #4: **E**motions Are Unacceptable

Negotiating is about logic and compromise, making sure everyone walks away from the table happy. There is no room for emotions, such as anger and impatience. You need to assess the deal from a businesslike standpoint, and if you become emotionally involved or try to win for the sake of winning, you may compromise the deal and its long-term benefits to you. Even if someone irritates you, keep your composure. Emotions should be kept off the negotiating table.

Rule #5: Respect Your Rival

Similar to rule #4, respecting your rival is critical to mutual negotiations. Even if you don't like your opponent, it's critical to remain respectful and refrain from insults. If you are not careful and resort to name-calling it can reveal a lot about your nature and even jeopardize your negotiations. Being disrespectful can never help, as you will cause extreme discomfort. Furthermore, you will ruin any chances of future deals, and the one thing you learn in life is that you never want to burn bridges—especially Golden Gate Bridges.

Rule #6: Honest Facts Only!

You might be tempted to lie about certain facts, helping your argument and case. However, you should be aware that lying on the negotiating floor is a dangerous route. When it is ultimately discovered that you lied—and, it will be discovered sooner or later—it can only hurt you and your argument. Your rival (and anyone else involved) will not trust you, causing you to lose credibility and damage your reputation. Do your research and find honest facts to support your argument, and you will be more respected because of it.

Rule #7: Offer Your Rival a Winning Solution

One of the best tactics to use when negotiating is to offer your rival a solution. Naturally, it has to benefit you in some way as well, but by offering solutions to how your rival can win, you will show you are making a goodwill effort to move the negotiations into a win-win position. Additionally, your rival will be more inclined to help you and offer you solutions as well once they see that you are interested in good fortune for everyone.

Rule #8: Understand the Other Party

One of the most critical steps in negotiating is understanding what the other party wants. This will be beneficial on many fronts. Firstly, it will show your rival that you are paying attention to what is important to them, gaining their favor—at least temporarily. Secondly, it will eliminate time and energy spent in circling fruitless solutions, ones that won't even be entertained by your rival. Third, once you know what is important to them, you can custom tailor your arguments and solutions for their problems. The bottom line is that you need to know what the other party wants, and once you determine it, you will be in the driver's seat.

Rule #9: Sacrifice Without Slaughtering—Compromising

Before you walk into the negotiating room, you must be prepared to compromise—even a little. It's not a sign of weakness or defeat. Rather, it is a tool to show the other party that you are willing to budge a little, in order to make the deal go through. However, it is easy to get caught up in sacrificing your position to a larger degree than necessary. Be knowledgeable of what you are willing to compromise, and where you draw the line. You can use your compromises as bargaining chips, only revealing them after every other argument is exhausted. By placing your compromises at strategic stages of the negotiation, you will ensure control over the situation.

Rule #10: Equipped to Walk Away

The final rule is to know when to walk away. Being able to leave the negotiating table is not easy, but you must mentally prepare yourself for this moment. If you have worn out all your arguments, proposed solutions, and compromises, it might be time to walk away from the negotiating table. You need to understand this reality even before you walk into the room. And if it comes down to it, you should not be willing to forfeit your goals just to make it work. Prepare yourself to leave everything behind without looking back, if you do indeed decide to end negotiations.

Chapter 1 Homework Reading—Recommended Books

Title: *How to Win Friends and Influence People*
Authors: Dale Carnegie, Arthur R. Pell
ISBN: 0671723650
Publisher: Simon & Schuster Adult Publishing Group

Title: *First Impressions: What You Don't Know About How Others See You*
Authors: Ann Demarais, Valerie White
ISBN: 0553803204
Publisher: Random House Group

Title: *Get the Interview Every Time: Fortune 500 Hiring Professionals' Tips for Writing Winning Resumes and Cover Letters*
Author: Brenda Greene
ISBN: 0793183022
Publisher: Dearborn Trade

Title: *60 Seconds and You're Hired!*
Author: Robin Ryan
ISBN: 0140289038
Publisher: Penguin Group

Title: *Getting to Yes: Negotiating Agreement Without Giving In*
Authors: Roger Fisher, William L. Ury, William Ury, Bruce Patton
ISBN: 0140157352
Publisher: Penguin Group

Chapter 1 Summary—The Least You Need to Know in Order to Pass the Class

1) When meeting someone for the first time, act genuinely interested in them—people like to feel important.

2) Be polite—yet assertive—when trying to contact people who are avoiding you. Just remember to tell them, "I'll be in your area and am planning to drop by," and see how quickly they call you back.

3) Use your resume as a legal bragging right to list everything you've accomplished, using action-oriented words.

4) Prepare for your interview by practicing with mock questions and doing plenty of research on the company.

5) Once the interview is over, put a thank-you note in the mail—even if you think the interview did not go well.

6) Win in negotiating by preparing properly, removing emotions from your arguments, and understanding what your rival wants.

CHAPTER 2—HOUSEHOLD ITEMS:
Home Sick

"Housework, if it is done right, can kill you."

—John Skow

Home Alone

When you are finally on your own for the first time, you may be intimidated by some of those "around the house" items. Have you gone through the stage of buying new underwear every two weeks because you are afraid of the whoosh-whoosh sound of the washing machine? Has a formal dinner gone awry when you used the fork to untie the triple knot in your shoe? Were you ever run over by a mad trucker and afraid to write a complaint letter?

In this chapter, you will learn how to:

- Wash, dry, and fold laundry

- Conduct yourself at a formal dinner

- Use the designated utensils for the correct dishes

- Write a complaint letter that gets results

- Go to the next level if the complaint letter is unanswered

I. How to Do Laundry

Laundry can be smelly. Laundry can be messy. Everyone knows laundry is dirty. The sad part is that laundry also has to get done. And the most affordable way is to do it yourself. Here's the breakdown on how to air your D.I.R.T.Y. laundry without *getting* dirty.

Determine What You Need

Identify Whites From Colors

Rinse and Wash

Transfer It Into the Dryer

Yikes! I Actually Have to Fold and Iron It?

Step #1: Determine What You Need

Quarters
The good old days of your mother washing your laundry is over. No more free lunch, no more free laundry. Depending on your laundromat, the price will vary, so be sure to call and ask ahead of time. You don't want to show up and start begging the homeless for quarters—because chances are, they don't have any either.

The Laundry Basket
Often overlooked, the laundry basket is quite helpful in helping you transport all your clothing to the Laundromat. You might like to carry a pile of laundry the size of Mt. Everest in your arms, barely being able to peek through the soiled socks and stained shirts, but take it on trust—the basket is easier.

Bleached!
A word of caution to those who have never done laundry in their lives: **bleach is only for white clothing!** If you are washing **only** white shirts, socks, and underwear, you might want to buy some bleach to add to the load. The bleach takes out marks on white clothing. But just remember, if you throw in bleach with colored

clothes, you'd better get used to blending in with the snow.

Fabric Softener

Although not necessary, fabric softener is used to make clothing a little softer and smell a little nicer. There are two types of fabric softener to choose from: one that is used during the wash cycle and one that is used in the dryer. You don't need it, but if you like to feel warm and fuzzy all over, spring for it.

Detergent Isn't Included

We live in a society where everything is included as a bonus. Well, not so with the washing machine. Contrary to what some of you may think, detergent isn't embedded inside the walls of the washing machine, so before you head out, you'll need to make a run to the local drugstore or supermarket to pick some up. Detergent comes in powder or liquid, and most of the time, it doesn't matter which you use. However, double check if the machine you are using has any special detergent requirements. Choose your weapon and head out— it's time to do the deed.

Step #2: Identify Whites From Colors

The Four Piles

Once you gather up the laundry, it is time to separate it. Make four separate piles: the whites, the darks, towels, and the items that are not washable. If you've never done laundry before and are wondering how to identify the items not washable, the best way to tell is by looking at the tag on the back of the garment. Usually, the tag will say something like, "Dry Clean Only." That would be a good indication that if you put your fluffy new red sweater into the washing machine, it will come out looking like a prune—or worse.

Whites vs. Darks

Ever wonder how your white socks turned pink when you were back in third grade, and your mom never told you? Well, here's how it happened. When you put colored clothing in the washing machine, part of the dye "bleeds" in the process, loosening the dye from the garment. That being the case, when you throw a white shirt into that same washing machine, the "bleeding dye" will stain the whites.

That's why it is imperative to separate your whites from your colors. Unless, of course, you prefer pink underwear.

The Neurotic Ones

For those of you who are neurotic, and think you must do a different load of laundry for *each* color (e.g. black, red, blue, etc.), chill out, because you don't need to. The dyes don't make any impact on dark colors, so you can lump an entire rainbow in there—without the whites. So lighten up, because if you don't, the laundry will.

Warning! Check Your Pockets!

During the process of separating the whites from darks, take the opportunity to check all pockets for loose change, important pieces of paper, dollar bills (20s if you have a big allowance), and make sure the clothes are not inside out (unless the label specifies otherwise).

Step #3: Rinse and Wash

The Stained Garments

If you have a shirt or other garment with a particular stain, place some detergent on the stain and rub it, before putting it into the washing machine. Doing so will help maximize the forceful and hard-hitting water effects of the washing machine. The stain might not come out, but it's a good tip to follow.

Why Are There So Many Cycles?

The simple answer is that not all clothing is created equal. Some clothing needs special treatment while other clothing is more flexible. Here's the breakdown on the different cycles and when to use them:

- Whites—These usually require a hot water cycle, as there is no "bleeding" that takes place with whites. The hot water cycle, as you can imagine, is usually more aggressive and swirls the clothing around with the attitude of a bully on a kindergarten playground.

- Darks—These usually require a warm or permanent press cycle. These cycles usually go easier on the clothing, adding cool water during the process. Think of it as the bully who has mercy on the kid with the broken leg—so he only takes *half* his money.

- Towels—Thicker in nature, they require setting the machine to a "heavy" load.

- Others—This is a cycle for more delicate and fragile garments. These garments (which are so sensitive, they're like a bully who politely asks you for your money), are usually taken to the dry cleaners but in the event that they are done in the washing machine, they usually require a cold cycle.

Operating the Washing Machine

This might be intimidating and scary, but just remember, using the washing machine is not like defusing a live bomb (and you know you could easily do that). Assuming the machine is a newer washing machine, place your smelly load of clothing into the machine (use a clothespin for your nose where applicable). Distribute the clothing evenly inside the machine to maximize results. Choose your applicable cycle (discussed above), and then pour in the detergent evenly onto your clothing. Close the door and finally insert quarters into the machine (if you're in a laundromat), and exhale deeply— you've finished phase one.

Warning #1: Don't Overstuff It!

Many first-timers think that a washing machine is like a suitcase— there's always room for a little more. If you do this, you'll possibly ruin your clothes and maybe even the machine. These machines are delicate, and therefore the machine should never be more than three-quarters full. If you find yourself with more clothing than that, do another load, cheapskate. It's better than burning out the motor and showing up on the local news as the "idiot who overstuffed a washing machine."

Warning #2: Using the Right Amount of Detergent

Using too little detergent won't be sufficient to get laundry clean. Using too much detergent can ruin your clothing, as well as cause a reenactment of the Biblical story of Noah's ark when the world flooded. Believe it or not, using too much detergent can cause massive overflow comparable to a bubble bath on steroids.

The Waiting Game

Most washing machines usually take between 20 and 40 minutes to complete a load, so you're going to have time to spare. Most people bring a book or walk around local shops to do some productive grocery shopping. Feel free to also sit on a bench and space out, or neurotically watch your laundry swirl round and round.

Step #4: Transfer It Into the Dryer

Hang-Ups

You may see some people who hang their washed clothing on a clothesline in their backyard. This might be effective assuming you live in a sunny part of town. But, if you're in Alaska during the winter, you might find the forthcoming advice on operating the dryer helpful.

The Fabric Softener

If you're using the fabric softener for the dryer, as discussed above, now is the time to whip it out of your bag of tricks.

Cleaning Up After Others

Somewhere in the dryer, close to the door (although it differs with each machine), there is a screen filter that is filled with lint and dirt. That's because all the people who used the machine before you were lazy and didn't want to empty it. In truth, emptying this filter is not crucial, but it is recommended for the best drying results. So buckle down, get the courage, and use a rubber glove if you have to—but empty the filthy filter.

Heating the Stains

Here's some information you need to remember: heat helps stains become permanently embedded. Knowing that information, it is important to take your clothing out of the washing machine and inspect those stains you were hoping to get out in the wash. If they didn't come out, you shouldn't put that garment into the dryer. Consider taking that one piece to professional cleaners to get rid of the stain.

The Waiting Game—Part II

Remember how you had to wait for the washing machine to finish? Well, get ready to do it again, as the average dryer can take up to an hour to complete a load. Grab that book or find your same warm spot on the bench—it's going to be a while.

Shrinkage

As you may already know, shrinkage happens. Cotton garments are more susceptible to shrinking, but this applies to all clothing. Beware that if you leave your clothing in the dryer for too long (meaning you spaced out and landed on another planet), the clothing may shrink to fit your Barbie and Ken dolls (there's nothing to be ashamed about; some people still play with their G.I. Joes).

Step #5: Yikes! I Actually Have to Fold & Iron It?

The Disappointment

Hooray! The dryer is done and your laundry is complete! Before you break out into a victory dance, take a deep breath, because there's one final piece to the puzzle. Unless you want to walk around looking like one big wrinkled prune, you're going to need to fold—and in some cases, iron—your clothing.

The Folding Game

Certain clothes need to be folded, while others can just be thrown into the drawer. Obviously, underwear and undershirts don't need to be ironed and crisply folded. But there are the other garments, like certain sweaters, jeans, pants, and sweatshirts, which need to be folded and placed into the closet. It's best to do the folding as soon as possible to minimize the number of wrinkles and crinkles.

What to Hang

Button-down shirts are the most common example of shirts that need to be placed on a hanger and hung in the closet. Some dress shirts are wrinkle-free and don't need to be ironed. But then there are the sensitive shirts that have so may wrinkles in them that they make your great-great-grandmother's skin look smooth. For those shirts and pants, you will need to use an iron to properly smooth them out.

Ironing is a hands-on process, and if you're committed to learning how to iron, watch someone else do it first (so if they mess up, it won't be on your clothing).

The Dry Cleaners
Cleaners usually do a nice job of ironing shirts for about $1 to $1.50 each shirt, and about $4 to $5 for pants. But if you're cheap and don't like ironing (like 99.9% of Americans), you should buy a majority of shirts and pants that are wrinkle free or wrinkle resistant, helping you simplify your laundry process. It's always nice to have a few dress shirts and pants for those fancy occasions (you know, when you're trying to show people that you're not homeless) but for all other times, those wrinkle-free shirts/pants will make your life much easier.

II. Dinner Etiquette

The Only Rule
There is only one genuine rule for dinner etiquette and table manners. Everything else is self-understood. Failing to put your napkin on your lap, spilling wine on the white tablecloth, and even picking up food with your fingers is all excusable. The only real rule you must abide by is to never, ever burp loudly. This is the loud and annoying belch you do without covering your mouth. It's repulsive, smelly, and downright disgusting to belch at another's table. But there is one kind of B.U.R.P. that is acceptable and encouraged:

Be Polite

Understand Your Utensils

Remove Disgusting Habits

Personalize the Ending

Step #1: **B**e Polite

Don't Be So Eager
The general rule of thumb is that the host should be the first to start. That means you don't sit at the table until the host sits. You don't put your napkin on your lap until the host does. You don't start eating until your host eats. But, if you have to use the restroom, you don't have to wait until your host does.

The Napkin Affair
Once you sit down, take your napkin and place it on your lap immediately. Do not tuck your napkin into the front of your shirt like a bib. Unless you prefer to give the image that you're ready to get down and dirty with those messy meatballs, place the napkin on your lap. Additionally, napkins, especially the cloth ones, are not meant to be used as tissues. If you have to blow your nose, excuse yourself to the restroom and pick a winner (use a tissue, please).

Butter Fingers

You're starved for a good meal, but when the meal begins with bread and butter, try to calm yourself. Don't put the butter directly from the main butter dish onto your bread. First, take a nice chunk of it and place it on your bread plate (if you have one). Then you can spread your butter from your own personal supply onto your bread. This helps keep your cooties away from the shared butter dish.

Oh, No! I Dropped My Fork!

It's okay, the world won't come to an end—unless you use the five-second rule. No matter how many seconds it was on the floor, don't pick it up and start eating with it like nothing happened. Simply apologize for causing any inconvenience and ask the host for a new one.

The Utensils Stay on Your Plate

When the actual meal begins and a utensil has touched your mouth, make sure that your utensils never touch the tablecloth again. They remain on the plate until it is cleared. Just imagine, do you think the host wants the residue of your saliva on his fancy tablecloth?

Step #2: Understand Your Utensils

Choose Your Weapons

Here's the basic setup of your utensils. Your plate is in the middle (duh), knife and spoon are on the right (with the knife edge facing your plate), and the forks (sometimes two or more) are on the left side of the plate. Your main drinking glass is at the top of your plate, toward the right-hand side. There are several slight variations, depending on the meal you're attending and the preferences of the host. But the above are the basic guidelines on how to decipher your utensils.

Which Fork Do I Use?

The general rule to follow is that the utensils farthest from the plate are used first. So for the salad appetizer, which will probably be the first course, use the fork farthest to the left. Then, as the next course continues, you move on to the next fork, and so on.

Eating Civilized

In the olden days, hunters shot animals, skinned them, and dragged them home for dinner. You can imagine that when it came time to cut the tender meat of cute little Lamb Chop, hunters stuck their knife into the meat like a dagger, and proceeded to chomp away at the poor lamb, ripping the meat from the bone with their bare teeth. Well, if you shot and killed the animal, you have full permission to use those manners. However, if you're like most people, there is a proper way to eat your food. To cut the tender meat (or anything else that you have the urge to cut), hold the fork in your left hand and the knife in your right, pointing the short edges of the fork downward. Place your index finger on the fork and knife, giving you more power over your utensils. Remember, you're not sawing a piece of wood, so be delicate with poor Lamb Chop. Gently cut off a piece of the meat and place it into your mouth. Be sure to chew with your mouth closed (if you ordered your meat rare, it may get scared and run for its life).

Step #3: Remove Disgusting Habits

The Main Ground Rules

As you can tell from this acronym, the worst possible thing you can do is let out a loud and disgusting belch during the meal. Not only is this nasty, it will probably get you kicked out way before dessert is served. So, if you like the meal so far, control yourself and don't let one out of your mouth.

The Slurping Syndrome

If one of the courses is soup, place the entire spoonful into your mouth, minimizing slurping. Slurping breeds the notion of a slob, one who is so famished and deprived of food, they can't take the extra second to eat politely.

Man's Worst Enemy

One final note about soup should be made. They're man's best friend, but when it comes to dining etiquette, they're man's worst enemy. As most of you know, dogs drink from their water bowl with their tongue, dripping drool and water from their hairy mouth afterward.

It looks like fun, but in a dinner setting, never drink directly from the edge of a bowl.

Remove Your Elbows
Elbows were not meant to be on the table. You can place your hands on the table, but not your elbows. No matter where this custom came into being, people will think you're a pig if you eat with your elbows on the table (do pigs even have elbows?).

Keep Your Mouth Shut
Remember the good old days, when you could eat, drink, talk, and burp all at the same time? Well, those days are over. You can never do all those things simultaneously again. In fact, it is considered especially rude to chew with your mouth open. Nobody wants to see how you've mangled poor Lamp Chop into road kill.

The Classic Spill
So you've spilled that hundred dollar glass of wine on the majestic white tablecloth. Instead of going into a hissy fit and calling 911, simply use your napkin to prevent the wine from dripping onto the person next to you and apologize for being clumsy. If you were unable to control the wine flow and it drips onto the beautiful blonde sitting to your right, control yourself. You might have the purest intentions when you dab your napkin on her blouse to remove the wine, but do yourself a favor and just offer to pay the dry cleaning bill. It will be a lot cheaper than a sexual harassment lawsuit.

Step #4: **P**ersonalize the Ending

Almost Over
You're almost there, so take a deep breath and get ready for the grand finale. Most people think that once dessert is over and the clock strikes 10, it's okay to let loose and make a beeline for the exit. If you care about making a good impression or being invited back, the ending is crucial.

How To Know When You're Finished
You may be wondering when the meal will end, assuming it is one of

those stiff and formal dinners. A clear indication that you are finished with your meal is when you place your knife and fork on the plate, with their points facing away from you. Once everyone else does the same, it is safe to place your napkin on the table, next to your plate. This will be another indication you are ready to get back to your messy room and your own set of dinner rules, where forks are replaced with toothpicks and the loudest belch wins a second beer.

Offer to Clean Up, You Pig: Non-Formal Occasions

Assuming you are in someone else's home, make the appropriate offer to help clean up. Usually, you will be told to relax and enjoy yourself. Despite this, you should bring in some of the dirty dishes from the dining room to the kitchen, as it shows your appreciation for the hospitality. Don't be too anxious, however, or you might find yourself in an apron with a dishtowel draped over your arm, scrubbing the dirty plates with a bacteria-filled sponge.

The Thank-You Note

Most people say good-bye, and never call or write again. Nobody will criticize you or think you are ungrateful. However, if you go out of your way to write a formal thank-you note (sorry, e-mail doesn't count), you will be invited back again (assuming you heeded all other advice above and didn't drink out of the soup bowl like a dog). People remember a nice touch like a personalized note, and in modern society, where good manners are hard to find, you'll stick out like white frosting on a dark chocolate cake.

III. Effective Complaint Letters

Everyone is upset about something. Whether it's about the waiter who dropped a hair in your soup, the Girl Scout who didn't make her own cookies, or the Sumo wrestler who fell out of the ring and broke your arm, knowing how to complain is critical. Regardless of the problem, there's a right way—and a wrong way—to complain about it. The right way to complain will get you satisfaction, results, and possible compensation. The wrong way will get you closer to an anger-fused heart attack. So, if you find yourself upset with a particular service or product, don't get mad. Just get C.R.A.N.K.Y.:

Charisma & Politeness Are Essential

Reasonable Requests Only

Attention: Mr. Important

Nitpick the Details

Know Your Ultimatum

Your Next Move (if No Initial Response)

Charisma & Politeness Are Essential

No Name-Calling
You know you want to call the company many names that include vulgarities, but it is wisest to call them by their real names. Calling someone Mr. Potato Head, Idiot-Who-Doesn't-Know-How-to-Run-a-Company, or Smelly, only ensures that you won't get a response from the person to whom you are writing. (unless his real name is Jim Sox, in which case "Smelly" is completely acceptable).

Anger Management
In a similar manner, you don't want to vent all your anger and frustrations onto paper. It's important to state the facts, but be sure not to get emotional about them. How will you know if your anger slithered its way into your letter? Read it to a friend or an unbiased

third party, asking them if it sounds to them like an "angry" letter. Another good indication that you're including your angry demeanor is if you break your keyboard by hitting the keys too hard.

The Blame Game

Don't place blame directly on the person to whom you are writing. Remember, the people reading your letter aren't the ones who dropped a nose hair into your burger. They're just the ones who *hired* the moron who did. It is, therefore, imperative not to make the blame personal.

Reasonable Requests Only

Be Rational

One of the essential elements of a complaint letter is requesting what you want in return. If you don't tell them what you want in your letter, they aren't going to grant it. However, the requests you make should be reasonable in nature. If you're complaining to a restaurant about the hair in your food, don't be a wise guy and ask for free meals for the next ten years. Asking for a simple meal is a reasonable request. (Unless that hair was especially long!)

What's Considered Reasonable?

Use the gift of common sense to determine what falls within the guidelines of reason, and what becomes ludicrous. If your last trip to the zoo was hindered when the monkey grabbed the banana from your hand, you could ask for free passes to the zoo. However, to request that a petting zoo be transported to your back yard would be stretching it just a bit.

Attention: Mr. Important

"To Whom It May Concern"

Those are the five most boring and ineffective words you could come up with when addressing a complaint letter. If that's who you address in your letter, you are showing that you didn't take the time to research who is in charge of the department. Without even continuing to read the letter, the reader will think the complaint really isn't that serious to you, since you didn't find out the appropriate contact person. All you need to do is call the company and ask the receptionist for the name of the person responsible for handling complaints and public relations. Address your letter to that person, and that extra step will help make you a more serious complainer.

Nitpick the Details

Details Paint a Picture

If something was legitimately wrong with the product or service, using details to explain what happened will paint a very descriptive picture. Naturally, you shouldn't write a thesis on what went wrong, but outlining the facts is always a good indication that your argument is valid. If you're upset that you ruined your new shoes because you stepped on a mushy banana, be sure to explain how it had absorbed into the sole of the shoe. However, a detailed explanation on the mushy banana texture—nobody wants the dissertation.

First Things First

Your very first sentence in your complaint letter should say exactly what the problem is and why. To continue the example from above, the following would be a good example of your opening sentence: "While strolling through public property, I stepped in your carelessly discarded mushy banana, which severely damaged my shoe and caused me to reinvent the term 'Slip N' Slide.'" Okay, maybe that's a little too far with the "Slip N' Slide" campaign, but the fact remains that you should open your letter with the problem and your specific complaint.

Know Your Ultimatum

Make Your Threats Real

If there's one thing everyone agrees on, it's that making threats you can't follow through with are not worth making. There's no point in threatening to burn down the chairman's house or kidnap his pet poodle, Fifi. Both the reader—and the writer—know those threats are phony, and won't be followed. Have a real ultimatum planned out in advance—such as taking the company to small claims court, contacting the media, involving your attorney, or simply not referring their product to any of your friends. Using the latter example certainly makes an impact when you inform them of your influential stature in the community (e.g. you're the president of the night-crawler research society, and have many friends in "dark" places).

The Clock Is Ticking

Did you ever notice that there is always a built-in clock ticking on your favorite action or drama TV show? "The bomb is going to go off in twenty-five minutes unless we stop it," or, "If we don't get her to a hospital within the hour, she's going to die!" It is not an accident or coincidence that you see this clock everywhere you turn. That's because with time ticking away, it builds an inherent tension with the audience. That's why you have to add a deadline in your complaint letter. So, when you conclude the letter, be sure to say that if you don't receive a response by a reasonable date, you will come after them with a hatchet and chain saw. (That last part is for effect—right?)

Your Next Move (if No Initial Response)

Next on the Food Chain

If the lousy good-for-nothing person you wrote to doesn't dignify you with a response, it's time to move up the food chain to the next person. You find out who this is by calling up the company yet again, and asking the lovely receptionist the name of the boss. It doesn't have to be the CEO, just the head of the department of the person who didn't respond to you. The person you initially contacted may not respect you, but he'll respect his boss. And, if you send the boss a letter saying that you initially contacted Mr. Scrooge, only to find him unresponsive to your complaint, rest assured that Scrooge will be on the verge of finding another job. Ultimately, you'll get what you want—a response and some positive action.

What if the Boss Doesn't Respond?

The first thing you should know is that this is rare. If you phrase your letter in a nice and respectable manner, chances are you're going to get a response from someone. However, it does happen from time to time that companies ignore you and won't respond to your complaint. That's when you take it to the next realm—maybe a regulatory board or an agency. If it's a doctor, there are governing agencies you can ask to get involved. The essential thing to remember is that once you get to the top authority—you'll eventually get to the bottom of the issue.

EXAMPLE OF A COMPLAINT LETTER

Background: What you are about to read below is a woman's complaint about mall security. You see, Ms. Bath dresses up as Santa during the holiday season in a local mall, and lets kids sit on her lap all day and night, telling her what they want for the holidays. It seemed like a safe job—until a kid pummeled poor Santa into the floor.

Brooke Linn
Chief of Security at Little Heaven Mall
1031 South Breakneck Street
Assawoman Bay, Delaware 10023

January 1, 2007

Dear Ms. Linn,

As the woman who dresses as Santa in the Little Heaven Mall, I was greatly disturbed last month when I was severely pummeled by a young hooligan, who somehow evaded the talented staff of security forces you have on call. The boy was unprovoked and clearly had mental problems. He forcefully threw his buff eight-year-old body into my chest, drop-kicking me to the ground. He proceeded to viciously attack me, ripping off my "beard" (the fake one, of course, because I am a woman and don't have a beard) and wind-milling his fists into my gut. This went on for approximately ten minutes, while the bystanders thought this was part of the scripted mall entertainment.

Your security staff, as I later discovered, was in the local doughnut shop, stuffing their bellies while mine was being punched. They were not at their posts where they should have been, and it is written in my contract that I will have security on call throughout the duration of my shift. It is disturbing and troubling to know the entire incident could have been prevented had your staff done their job.

I am requesting that you do a thorough investigation of your department, interrogating the officers on duty while I was being attacked. I also request that I be given protective gear, so that this will never happen again. I would like a bullet proof vest, cup (yes, the kind you wear on your private parts), in addition to a Billy club, slingshot, automatic machine-gun, bazooka, and handcuffs. I will expect to hear back from you no later than February 1, 2007. If I do not receive a response by that time, I will have no choice but to contact your superiors and involve my attorneys, who are receiving a carbon copy of this letter.

I take pride in the work I do, and hope that you will do the same. I enjoy making children laugh and have fun, and because of your negligent security staff, one little punk has put me in this wheelchair and body cast. I trust that you will ensure this never happens again to me, or to any of the other Santas, Easter bunnies, and clowns that work in the Little Heaven Mall.

My address is listed above, and I can be contacted via phone at 555-537-8008. I look forward to hearing from you.

Warmest Regards,

Anita Bath

Chapter 2 Homework Reading—Recommended Books

Outwitting Housework: *Tips, Tricks, and Advice*
Authors: Nancy H. Rosenberg, Laurie Heidorn
ISBN: 1592283497
Publisher: Lyons Press, The

Title: *If It's Broke, Fix It!*
Authors: Dan Ramsey, Judy Ramsey
ISBN: 1592571034
Publisher: Penguin Group

Title: *Lady at the Table: A Concise, Contemporary Guide to Table Manners*
Authors: Sheryl Shade, John Bridges, Bryan Curtis
ISBN: 1401601774
Publisher: Rutledge Hill Press

Title: *Everyday Letters for Busy People: Hundreds of Samples You Can Adapt at a Moment's Notice*
Authors: Deborah Hart May, Regina McAloney
ISBN: 1564147126
Pub. Date: December 2003

Title: *Send This Jerk the Bedbug Letter: How Companies, Politicians, and the Mass Media Deal with Complaints and How to Be a More Effective Complainer*
Author: John Bear
ISBN: 0898158117
Publisher: Ten Speed Press

Chapter 2 Summary—The Least You Need to Know in Order to Pass the Class

1) Make four separate piles when doing laundry: whites, darks, towels, and items that are not washable.

2) Use a hot cycle for whites, warm/permanent press cycle for darks, and cold water (or maybe even the professional dry cleaners) for sensitive clothing.

3) The dryer forces a stain to become embedded into clothing.

4) If you are unsure of what to do during dinner, wait to see what the hosts do, and imitate them.

5) Table manners and thanking the host after dinner (with a thank-you note) are of key importance.

6) Write complaint letters to the attention of the correct person, using polite language, reasonable requests, and details of the situation.

7) If the complaint letter does not yield a response, contact the person's boss, and if still unresponsive, go to regulatory agencies to report them.

CHAPTER 3—PRESENTATIONS:
Speech-Less

"Why doesn't the fellow who says, 'I'm no speechmaker,' let it go at that instead of giving a demonstration?"

—Kin Hubbard

The Fear Factor

Once you leave school, there will be a variety of occasions where you might have to deliver a presentation or speech. These include work situations, weddings, and other social affairs. People have two major fears: flying and public speaking. Unfortunately, you're on your own with the flying phobia. However, public speaking and speech preparation are a different story. You'll hear many common tips on how to deliver a speech, such as eating healthy beforehand, getting enough sleep the night before, and imagining the audience naked. Depending on your audience, this may actually trump the fear of flying. Considering the fact that roughly 99% of the human race are not supermodels, don't imagine your audience naked. Don't show up naked, either. But *do* think N.A.K.E.D.

In this chapter, you will learn how to:

- **N**ever Mismatch the Audience & Subject Material
- **A**rrange the Structure
- **K**eep It Simple Stupid—How to Write It
- **E**ntertain Your Friends (& Other Practice Methods)
- **D**eliver It

I. Never Mismatch the Audience & Subject Material

Knowing the Audience
This is a pretty simple step in the process, but if you mess it up, your entire speech will blow up in your face. If you're speaking at an animal rights seminar, don't speak about how you admire your talented local butcher for getting all the blood out of the red meat. This may seem like a ridiculous rule to follow, but find out who you are speaking to first before deciding what subject matter to discuss.

Investigate Your Listeners
Don't do background checks on all 50 people attending your speech, because that would make you neurotic, and in some circles, a stalker. However, research the type of audience you will be speaking to. Is this an audience that likes to participate? What are they expecting from your speech? To be informed or entertained? Do they like to laugh? Cry? Ask questions? You can find out the answers to these important questions by speaking with the individual who asked you to speak or people who have gone to similar events in the past.

II. Arrange the Structure

The Overall Structure
With every novel, movie, and fairy tale, there is a beginning, middle, and end. A speech shares those same elements. However, as opposed to a movie, where you have different people who are story editors, writers, directors, and actors, you are everybody rolled into one when it comes to speechwriting. You have to organize, write, and deliver it all by yourself (unless you're the President of the United States, who has a stable of staff writers, in which case you wouldn't be reading this book). This is the part of the process where you have to organize and arrange the structure of your speech.

How Long Should It Be?
To quote my father, "The best speech is a short speech." Enough said.

The Introduction

You only get one chance for a first impression, so make it good. Here are a few tips on a successful opening:

- **Why Did the Chicken Cross the Road?**—Don't use this one, but a joke that's funny, appropriate, and more importantly, relevant, will help ease the crowd a bit. These jokes can be one-liners, Q&As, or stories. But whatever you do—don't use the chicken joke.

- **Ask a Question**—Don't ask them for their Social Security number, or whether the men prefer boxers or briefs (unless you're speaking at an underwear convention), but a striking first question related to your topic may be the quickest and most effective way of captivating the audience's attention.

- **Story Time**—Beginning with a personal story helps relate you to the audience. Instead of speaking **at** them, suddenly you are speaking **to** them. It can be a comical story or a sad one, but whatever it is, it should relate back to your subject matter and the point about which you are going to speak.

- **The Hook**—There are many other creative and inventive ways to start off a speech, such as making a bold and mysterious statement or hiding the identity of the famous person you are talking about until the end. The most important aspect of your opening is getting the audience interested and captivated by what you are about to say.

The Main Body

This is the meat and potatoes of your speech. You have captivated your audience and tapped into their 5-second attention span, dragging it on for what seems to be forever. Here are some tips on how to organize and structure your main body:

- **Make an Outline**—Go back to first grade, where they taught you the alphabet and how to count. Use the letters of A, B, and C to head your main points, and then subcategories of 1, 2, and 3 to go into more detail of what your main topics are all about. Just in case a few of you missed this technique in school, here's an example for a speech on how to care for your pit bull named Hooch:

    A. Walk Hooch Twice Daily
        i. Bring pooper scooper
           1. How to avoid the neighbors' wrath
           2. Story of when Hooch had bowel issues
       ii. Make sure leash is securely attached to collar
           1. Story of when Hooch broke loose and bit someone's toe off
    B. Hooch's Monthly Bath
        i. How to get his collar off without taking your hand with it
       ii. Types of shampoo/conditioner Hooch prefers
           1. Baby shampoo works best, preventing his eyes from tearing

- **Sprinkle Your Speech With Goodies**—With each topic you cover, be sure to include stories (even if they're not your own), analogies, anecdotes, and other "goodies" to keep the audience interested. These little treasures help keep your audience interested and focused during the main body of your speech. Use them often enough, and you'll keep them interested up until the very end.

The Conclusion

Most people think all the work is done at this point and you can cruise into the sunset. Sorry to break the news to you, but the conclusion is arguably one of the most important parts of the speech. It can make or break you—even if you've dominated the speech until this point. To have a powerful conclusion, use these pointers:

- **Summarize Your Main Points**—Each topic and area that you spent time on should be summarized in a maximum of one sentence. So, if you spoke about five methods of how to beat up your kid sister, summarize each of those methods, totaling five sentences. If you practice enough, you will probably be able to condense it into two or three sentences, which is more preferable. Make all your summary sentences into a nice, flowing paragraph. This will help keep your audience focused on your material.

- **The Final Sentence**—This is where you leave them laughing, intrigued, and begging for more. The final sentence **must** be prepared prior to your delivery, and should be witty, smart, and possibly funny, depending on your topic and audience. Don't underestimate the importance of the final sentence, because if you do, it might really be the final sentence you ever say in public.

Research First, Structure Later

Remember, just because you start with an introduction, spend most of the time on your main body, and finish with a conclusion doesn't mean you have to research it in that order. Start off doing the research on your main body *first,* as that will allow you to be focused and knowledgeable on your topic. Only at the end are you truly "qualified" to search for a dynamic introduction. So research first, and then organize it into the proper structure later.

III. Keep It Simple Stupid—How to Write It

It's Easy, Sorta

Writing your now-structured speech will be easy, considering you have it organized and know what you want to say. Without the proper organization and structure in the previous step, writing your speech will be like climbing Mount Everest barefoot—difficult and agonizing. However, actually cranking out the words onto paper can be a challenge at times. Just remember, the better organized structure you have, the easier it will be to actually write it.

Don't Use SAT Words

Besides the very few brainiacs in the audience, nobody is really interested in hearing your version of the microbiology thesis that only a handful of Harvard graduates could understand. Unless this is intended to be a speech laden with ornamental words, stay far away from them. You want your audience's eyes on you—not in a dictionary.

The Thesaurus Is Your New Friend

On one hand, you don't want to use fancy words, on the other hand, you want to use a variety of words. A speech can get stale and boring if the speechmaker uses the same words. The thesaurus can be very helpful in this situation. Make sure you're using different—but not difficult—words (did you notice how many times the same "word" was used?), and your audience won't think you sound like a broken record...broken record...broken record.

Remember to Sprinkle

As you go through the writing phase, be sure to include the little one-liners or anecdotes mentioned above. Even if they are not in your outline, add in some humor (if appropriate, of course), or other little goodies to make it entertaining.

The Note Card Syndrome

For some people, reading off a piece of paper is not in their best interest, as they won't have a podium or place to rest their papers. In such a case, index or note cards become helpful. The only item to be aware of is called the "Note Card Syndrome." Ever see those guys giving speeches, and it looks like they've got a kink in their neck because they're constantly staring downward? That's because their eyes are glued to the note cards in their hands. So, if you're going to do this, be careful not to fall into the trap of the Note Card Syndrome.

IV. Entertain Your Friends (& Other Practice Methods)

Practice, Practice, Practice!

In case you didn't understand the headline, the key to an effective speech is to practice it. Even the most polished, professional, and seasoned speakers practice their speech *multiple* times before delivering it. There's no need to take a leave of absence from school or work in order to practice, but give yourself adequate time to rehearse it properly.

Tape Record Yourself

It may seem trivial, but using a tape (or video) recorder can help you discover if you are speaking too quickly or too slowly, stuttering, or sounding like a robot. Most people enjoy hearing the sound of their own voice, so here's a chance to do just that—and actually gain something from it.

Mirror, Mirror, On the Wall. . .

This works well for some and is torturous for others. Practicing your speech in front of a mirror can be helpful, especially if you notice you have a booger hanging from your left nostril. But other times it can be distracting, as you are more interested in how your hair looks than how your voice projection and speech gestures are flowing. The mirror works well for some, but not for all. Only use it if it helps—and spotting that hanging booger before you speak can be quite helpful.

Ad Lib

This means to improvise and deliver parts of the speech extemporaneously. This is only effective when you are confident about the subject matter you are talking about, and you have the audience in a captivated mood. This means you don't have the exact words mapped out on paper, and it sounds like it is flowing more naturally than a mechanical sentence. It can help to ad lib (only a few sentences at a time) during your practice time, as you might even surprise yourself when you actually deliver the speech.

Raising Your Voice Does Not Mean Shouting

When you are about to make an important point in the speech, consider raising your voice—which is not the same as shouting—to a tone that is louder than the rest of the speech. Likewise, lowering your voice—which is not the same as whispering—can also have the same effect. Just be sure that when you raise your voice, you don't scare your audience.

Eye Contact

This is possibly one of the hardest public speaking techniques to master. Looking people in the eye can be intimidating. But worse than intimidating, eye contact can bring on an onslaught of unexpected problems. Everyone knows that the eyes are in close proximity to the mouth, nose, and ears. When speakers look an audience member in the eye, they might be distracted by drool dripping down a chin, an ugly pimple that should have been popped three weeks ago, and a nose hair protruding into public airspace. Do your best to make eye contact (and **only** look at their eyes). But, if the audience is a bunch of slobs, do your best to look up at something else, like the exit sign, wall clock, or back doors. That nose hair will scar you for life.

Physical Gestures
Hand motions and physical gestures are important during a speech, but you also have to know your limit in using them. Using your hands to illustrate a point can be a key component, since the audience will then know that you have fully functioning limbs—as opposed to keeping them hidden behind the podium. But be careful not to flap your arms excessively. People might think you're pretending to be a bird and fly away (and if that really is your intention, you might want to consider going south for the winter).

V. Deliver It

Get Plenty of Rest
Expect to be nervous the night before. Tums will calm your stomach, but you have to focus on getting a sufficient amount of sleep. Walking in front of your audience with blood-shot eyes, a stiff neck, and a woozy gaze might not give the right impression.

Physical Appearance
Remember that hanging booger you noticed while practicing your speech? Just make sure it isn't there when you're about to go center stage. Be sure that your hair is combed, your shirt is pressed, and your chest hair is sufficiently tucked away.

Smile!
You might feel like there is an Alien vs. Predator war going on in your stomach, but do your best to smile on the outside. People who appear happy, confident, and positive are well received by the audience even before the speech begins. And, if you notice someone smiling at you with a little twinkle in their eyes, be careful. They might want

something more than a good speech.

Calm Your Liver!

Getting up in front of an audience is intimidating and scary—especially for the first time. Keep in mind that the audience forms their first impression within the first few seconds of seeing you. That being the case, you have groomed yourself properly and are smiling from cheek to cheek, right? This can be an enormous advantage, as you will be getting positive vibrations from the entire room even before the speech begins. Plus, the best way to give an effective speech is by preparing for it properly. And if you've been following every step before this one, you'll be on your way to delivering a dynamic speech.

Mistakes Are Acceptable

Everyone makes mistakes in public speaking. The deciding factor is how you handle those mistakes and what you do about them. If you mispronounce a word, simply say it correctly and move on. If you accidentally skipped a paragraph in your speech, just keep going and move on. But, if your pants or skirt fall down and you ran out of clean underwear yesterday, don't just move on. First, pull it up, apologize—and *then* move on. The audience will respect you for taking charge of the situation when mild blunders happen (but just for the record, dropping your trousers or skirt isn't mild).

Chapter 3 Homework Reading—Recommended Books

Title: *10 Days to More Confident Public Speaking*
Authors: Lenny Laskowski, Philip Lief Group Staff,
Princeton Language Institute Staff
ISBN: 0446676683
Publisher: Warner Books, Incorporated

Title: *Motivating Your Audience: Speaking to the Heart*
Authors: Hanoch McCarty, William D. Thompson
ISBN: 0205268943
Publisher: Pearson Education

Title: *The Quick and Easy Way to Effective Speaking: Modern Techniques for Dynamic Communication*
Authors: Dale Carnegie, Dorothy Carnegie
ISBN: 0671724002
Publisher: Simon & Schuster Adult Publishing Group

Title: *Public Speaking For Dummies*
Author: Malcolm Kushner
ISBN: 0764559540
Publisher: Wiley, John & Sons, Incorporated

Title: *What to Say for Every Occasion: Model Speeches, Letters, and Remarks*
Author: David Belson
ISBN: 1567315410
Publisher: Barnes & Noble Books

Chapter 3 Summary—The Least You Need to Know in Order to Pass the Class

1) Research the type of audience you will be speaking to, determining if they like to laugh or cry; whether they like to participate or take a passive role.

2) Outline your speech into a beginning, middle, and end, using hooks to draw the audience in. Combine it with stories, jokes, and anecdotes in the middle to keep them interested.

3) Make your speech easy to understand, summarizing main points and staying away from hard-to-understand words.

4) Use many tools to practice your speech, including friends, a tape recorder, and the mirror.

5) Get enough sleep the night before the speech. Smile, use hand gestures where appropriate, and allow for mistakes to occur without panicking.

CHAPTER 4—APARTMENTS & HOMES:
Home-A-Loan

"Why do they call them apartments when they're close together?"

—Author Unknown

Crybaby

This is it, the big day. Your parents watched you graduate kindergarten, grade school, and then high school. They cried with every step you took, but nothing will prepare them—or you—for the grand event of moving to a place of your own. Moving to a new city is emotionally, physically, and financially draining. If you've got a special blankie you hold onto for comfort, now's the time to grab it. (Don't worry, your secret is safe. Some people need theirs until they get married.)

In this chapter, you will learn how to:

- Research and find the best apartments available

- Inspect the premises and ask the right questions

- Survive the process of buying a house

- Choose the right mover for your situation

- Organize your belongings a month, two weeks, and the day of your move

I. The Apartment Complex

Finding your dream apartment may not be as easy as crashing in your college dorm room, but it could also have many fringe benefits. Just think: no dorm counselor (although there is a landlord), no curfew (except the annoying old man upstairs), and no cramped quarters (unless you're in NYC). Well, maybe the college dorm was more fun but, unfortunately, you can't live in one forever. There are four basic steps to finding your very own C.R.I.B.:

Calculate How Much It Will Cost

Research & Find an Apartment

Inspect the Premises

Biting the Bullet & Signing the Lease

Step #1: Calculate How Much It Will Cost

What to Expect
Let's talk money. You've got to know how much you can afford *before* you go apartment hunting. Your allowance from your parents, bimonthly paycheck, or lottery winnings will determine how much you can afford to spend on an apartment. Once you have that determined, you'll know what you can afford—and what you can dream about.

Money Up Front
This is the part that makes everyone cringe. Landlords are very greedy people when it comes to money up front. Before you move in, they will usually require that you put down a security deposit, the *first* month of rent, the *last* month of rent, and a broker fee. If you completed second grade math, you realize by now that this is four separate payments—and you haven't even moved in yet!

Credit Check
Your credit background will mean a lot to a landlord. They will do a

financial background check on you, determining if you've paid your bills on time or have outstanding loans, and other selected financial information. As a quick reference point, the three biggest credit agencies where you can check your own credit are Equifax (www.equifax.com), Transunion (www.transunion.com), and Experian (www.experian.com).

Broker? Who the Heck Is a Broker?

In true layman terminology, a broker is a matchmaker. He puts a buyer and seller together, usually taking a small percentage of the fee, to cover his time and expense. It's usually the larger cities that have brokers (e.g. New York, Los Angeles, Miami), while smaller cities won't use them (e.g. Last Change, CO; Slaughter, LA; Horseheads, NY; and Mud Lick, KY).

Don't Be Stingy

If you are using a broker, just remember that you don't have to limit yourself to one. They only get paid if they make the deal, so don't be afraid to have multiple brokers at the same time. Additionally, when talking to a broker, be sure to downplay how much you can afford. For example, if you can realistically afford $1000 a month, be sure to tell them you can't afford a penny over $750. Rest assured, the brokers will come back to you—regardless of the price you give them—with a few hundred dollars higher, saying that's all they have available. This is why there aren't many brokers in the very friendly city of Slaughter, Louisiana.

Step #2: Research & Find an Apartment

Where to Find It

There are a variety of places to find an apartment, but here are a few of the most common methods to jump-start your search.

1. Internet—Finding an apartment has never been easier online. Simply scour the appendix for a listing of countless web sites that feature apartments in virtually every major city.

2. Drive By—Use your scouting skills by driving through neighborhoods of your choice, looking for signs that say

apartments are available. However, most people merely get the phone number and call. Take a more proactive approach and go into the building and knock on the landlord's door. Most of the time, landlords get so many phone calls a day, they often don't call back! That being the case, muster up the courage and knock on the landlord's door unannounced. One note of caution: if you knock on the landlord's door at 4 a.m., you'll probably be greeted by a shotgun instead of a sales pitch.

3. The Classifieds—These can be good places to find apartments in areas you would never think to look. See the appendix with a full listing of Web site services that can help you find places to rent. The best part? Most of these services are free.

4. Message Boards—Check out different newsgroups and local message boards for people who are not as inclined to list their places in classifieds, but have availability postings on the message boards.

5. Word of Mouth—Your mother's cousin's sister's aunt probably knows one of the Martians who landed from outer space, and has the perfect apartment you are looking to rent! So don't be shy and hide your enthusiasm about finding an apartment. Spread the word, and who knows, you might get an apartment that's truly out of this world.

What To Bring

If you are serious about an apartment, the items to bring with you are printouts of your credit report, references (from your old landlord, if you had one), your driver's license, and cash equivalents (e.g. a cashier's check or a money order). Make a mental note that in this regard, landlords don't take credit cards or personal checks. They want to know they are getting their money and, therefore, are very particular about what they will accept.

Step #3: Inspect the Premises

What to Look for

Obviously, there are two parts to the apartment—the outside and the inside. Some of you may not care what the outside looks like as long as it has running water and four walls (you'd be surprised what people call "walls" these days). But be sure to consider some of the exterior factors as well.

On the Outside

1. General Upkeep—Notice if the lawn outside the building is neatly kept, or if there are thorns and shrubbery growing out of control. Also ask about general items, such as storage rooms and security. The last thing you want is to come home and wear protective armor just to get into your building.

2. The Common Areas—Look at places like the elevator, hallways, lobby, car garage (don't forget to check for guest parking availability!), recreation facilities (e.g. pool) and laundry room. Because if it's more than just dirty laundry stinking up the laundry room, it says something about the landlord's policy in keeping the building clean.

3. The Lock on Your Door—Technically this is part of the inside of the apartment, but for this purpose, categorize it as an exterior feature. That's because of who you're trying to keep *out*. Take note of whether the door is a deadbolt or chain, and if it is sturdy enough to do its job. Some deadbolt locks are old and warped, making it excruciatingly difficult to lock your door. So, when you check out the room, pretend it's Friday the Thirteenth, and test your lock.

On the Inside

Below is a room-by-room checklist, making it easy for you to navigate your way through the apartment, looking for the most important things.

Living Room & Dining Area

1. Electric Outlets—Make sure there are enough outlets, since this is most likely the place where you will plug in your TV, cable outlet, arcade games, and neon signs. It's not enough to see them—make sure they are working.

2. Phone Jacks—You might want to have a phone in this room to order one of those rip-off items from a late-night infomercial.

3. Space—Is there enough room to set up your couch, kitchen table, TV, wall unit, motorcycle, pet lion, and any other items/creatures you plan on keeping in there?

4. Wall Paint—Is the paint a fresh coat or is it chipping away? Just imagine sitting there watching your favorite TV show with a glass of water—when suddenly, a paint chip from your wall falls into it. Not something you would see on the Food Network.

5. Lighting—Notice if there are overhead chandeliers or, at the very least, spaces to have lamps. It would be a bummer to bring home a date and be left in the dark.

The Kitchen

1. Electric Outlets—Once again, crucial for cooking, regardless of how much or little you cook. Even boxed macaroni and cheese requires a stove.

2. The Cabinets—Open each and every one of them, using a flashlight to inspect the back corners. You never know what you might find, including mouse droppings (that isn't a joke).

3. Refrigerator—Does the apartment come with one or do you have to supply it yourself? If one is already there, see if you can modify the temperature to your liking or if the dial is permanently stuck on "Ice Age."

4. The Square Footage—Bring a tape measure, pad, and pen so

you can measure how wide and long the space is to fit a kitchen table. All you need to do is jot down the numbers, so when you go shopping for a kitchen set, you'll know what the parameters are. The last thing you want to do is buy a kitchen table and chairs, and realize that you can only fit three out of the four chairs into the kitchen—and the fourth will be halfway into the bathroom. Not a bad deal if you invited "obligatory" visitors (you know, like relatives and other annoying house guests), and wish you could flush them down the toilet.

5. The Stove—Ask if it is electric or gas. And, if it's gas, ask if there have been any leaks recently. (For those of you not familiar with the difference between gas and electric stoves, you probably won't be interested in the kitchen portion of the apartment anyway.)

Bathrooms

1. Flush the Toilet—No, it's not necessary to do anything in it beforehand, but you should take note to flush the toilet and see if it makes any strange sounds, is leaky, or appears to come close to overflowing.

2. Use the Sink—Similar to the toilet, turn the water on (both hot and cold), to make sure it is functioning properly. Notice if there is a steady stream of water, or if it is sputtering with brown and black water (for those with poor hygiene, take note that this would be a bad sign).

3. Go Undercover—Open the cupboard below the sink while the faucet is on, and examine the pipes below. You don't need to be a plumber to know that rusty and leaky pipes are the start of a mini flood. Be sure to bring your Rubber-Ducky!

Bedrooms

1. Electric Outlets—You're going to need plugs for all sorts of things, like clock radios, treadmills, and battery chargers for your stun gun.

2. Spacing—Use your tape measure to judge if you will be able to fit your bed, desk, dresser, and any other furniture into the room. If you're short on space, you might want to get creative and use one item for several purposes (e.g. hanging underwear on your bedpost).

3. Carpet or Tile—Is the floor of the bedroom carpet, wood, or tile? You might not care now when you have shoes on, but just wait until a cold night when you suddenly have the urge to use the restroom.

4. Windows—Open and close the windows and/or shades to make sure they work properly. There's nothing worse than trying to get some sleep with that nosy owl watching you from the window.

5. The Wall Thickness—It will be hard to tell, but do your best to determine how thick/thin the walls are between rooms—and apartments. You might want to get into bed early, but a rock drummer who starts his day (or night, in this case) at 11 p.m., will make things a little noisy.

6. Closet Space—Note if there is enough room for your clothing, or if you will need to buy an extra dresser to accommodate your wardrobe.

7. Ceiling—Look for stains in the ceilings of each room, which can be an indication of leaks.

Step #4: Biting the Bullet & Signing the Lease

Down to Business

1. Once you've fully inspected the apartment and are relatively satisfied with the premises, here are a few additional issues to cover with the landlord.

2. Deposit—Virtually every landlord requires a deposit upfront. What will they be charging?

3. Smoke Detector—Make sure your apartment has a smoke detector and find out the last time it was checked.

4. Minimum Term—What is the minimum term of the lease, and how much could it be raised thereafter?

5. Clean It Up—Ask the landlord to do a full cleaning (e.g. carpet cleaning, paint job, etc.) of the apartment right before you move in.

6. Security—This may not be the biggest concern, but it's always nice to know if there are cameras watching the front lobby.

7. Parking—Find out where people park their cars and if there is an additional cost for a parking spot in the building (if applicable).

8. Pets—Some apartments allow pets while others prohibit them. Be sure to find out before you haul in your aquarium tank and shark to your new crib.

Signing the Lease

Leases can be intimidating if you're looking at one for the first time. Every lease will have slightly different terminology, but here are the main points you should understand in your *written* lease:

1. Term/Length—Be sure it specifically states how long the term of the lease is. You don't want a month-to-month agreement, as the landlord can astronomically raise the rent or worse, kick you out because Tony the Mobster made the landlord a deal he couldn't refuse.

2. Rent Control—Some states have this law, which means that landlords can only increase your rent by a maximum percentage (usually around 2%) each year. Regardless of whether your state has this law or not, be sure to have a clause in the lease stating what the maximum is for increases.

3. Who's Responsible—Have it clearly laid out who is responsible for fixing things in the apartment should things fall apart. If your shower suddenly stops working, you don't want to hear your landlord say, "There's clean water in the toilet bowl, isn't there?"

4. Bring in the Crew—Make sure the lease clearly states that your apartment will be cleaned and evaluated for damage (e.g. leaky faucet or stained carpet) before your arrival.

5. Put Everything Important in Writing—No matter how small it is, if it's important to you, get it in writing in the lease. If the landlord promises to give you free cable, put it in the lease. If they promise they'll never come in unannounced, put it in writing (unless you like unexpected visitors at 4 a.m.). No matter what it is—make sure it's clearly documented.

II. Home Owe-ner

The Big Leagues
So here you are, the big man on campus, and you are going to buy a house. Most people right out of school aren't heading to Beverly Hills to buy a 25-million-dollar mansion. With that in mind, this portion of the book is an abbreviated overview of buying a home. It's an attempt to familiarize you with the process, terms, and information that most people don't learn for many years after college. So, after reading this, you might not be ready to buy a house on your own, but you'll be knowledgeable enough about the game to play it when the time comes around.

The First Step
You need to know how much you can afford. This is one of those areas where you can't exaggerate or stretch the truth. Maybe your Uncle Joe really climbed Mount Everest naked, and maybe you're really the one who invented Google, but when it comes to deciding how much to pay for your home, you've got to be honest with yourself. Keep in mind that the expenses you will incur include a down payment, closing costs, insurance, taxes, and, of course, your monthly mortgage. Take a deep breath and exhale slowly, it's not as bad as you think (unless your Uncle Joe really did climb that mountain naked).

The Down Payment
Banks know that if a house costs $300,000, chances are you won't be able to pay cash up front for the whole amount (unless you work with some very influential people). Therefore, the customary down payment for the homebuyer is 20% of the house price. The rest of the money will be lent to you by a financial institution, such as a bank, and interest will be charged on that borrowed money. This remaining amount of money that you must pay back to the bank is called your mortgage, and is paid on a monthly basis. You have the option of choosing a myriad of payment plans, such as 15 or 30-year mortgages. Thirty years is a long time down the road (you may even be a grandparent by then—GASP!), but those are the usual provisions that come with a mortgage.

The Under-20% Lure

You will hear commercials for mortgages with 100% financing. That means you put no money (or under 20%) as your down payment, and they lend you 100% of the money! Warning! Remember what you were taught in first grade: if it's too good to be true, it usually is. If you get 100% financing, very often your interest rate will be hiked up very high, and in some situations, the financial institution lending you the money will force you to take out Private Mortgage Insurance. Although not conclusive, a general monthly ballpark figure for Private Mortgage Insurance is $45 per every $100,000 mortgage (e.g. if you have a $300,000 mortgage, Private Mortgage Insurance is $135 per month). As you can imagine, this all starts to add up to a pretty penny (and from any angle, it isn't pretty).

It's a PITI

This is one of those terms that's ironic—and not funny. PITI stands for Principal, Interest, Tax, and Insurance. Note that no matter where you live, you will have to pay all these elements. However, in some states, they combine all four items to calculate your monthly mortgage payment. It really is a "pity" that they couldn't come up with a better name.

A Little Deceiving—Tack on the Extras

Most people think that when they see a home with a price tag of $300,000, their monthly mortgage will be based on the interest payments of $300,000. This can be somewhat deceptive, as that does not take into account the tax and insurance payments (in the PITI acronym above), not to mention the little repairs here and there. All these items add up, and although this is discouraging news, it's important you know this before looking for a home—not after you've purchased it.

Finding the Home of Your Dreams

Scouting out your new house can takes weeks, months, even years. There are many places to go home hunting, ranging from Web sites, to magazines, to ads in the newspapers. It's pretty easy to get overwhelmed with all the types of homes on the market, but here are a few pointers to remember when searching for your new home:

1. Crime Rate of Neighborhood—Can you see yourself being

outlined in chalk in your new home? If so, keep looking.

2. Closeness to Work—Will you need a private helicopter to take you to and from work every day? Stop daydreaming, it will never happen!

3. Closeness to the City—Is the grocery store close by? Do you care?

4. Taxes—Some places have both a city and a county tax, so beware of where you are standing—it might be the place they come to handcuff you if you can't pay your taxes.

5. Noisy Neighbors—Is the home near a college campus or a cemetery? Remember, cemeteries make very quiet neighbors.

The Real Estate Agent

Sometimes you love them and sometimes you hate them, but they are a pretty important part of buying a house. The agent is usually a super friendly, always-smiling individual who is familiar with the property and can tell you all the details about it. They also act as the middleman between you and the seller. Think of them as an undercover operative working for the seller. They get paid based on a percentage of how much the home sells for. So it's in their best interest to get the highest dollar amount possible. Once you make an offer, you usually tell the agent who will, in turn, tell the seller. It seems like a lot of games to play, but if you were to deal with the seller directly, it could get ugly. There are rare times that you can negotiate the deal on your own without a real estate agent, but it is infrequent.

The Double Agent

Why does the buyer have to deal with an agent who is working undercover for the seller? Isn't that just unfair? Indeed, it is. Which is why there are double agents. Their real name is the Buyer's Agent, and as you guessed, they work for the buyer—not the seller. Buyer's Agents get paid either by an hourly rate, flat fee, or a commission of the selling price, but regardless of how they get paid, they are on your side. It might be a little more costly upfront to use a Buyer's Agent, but in the end, they could save you thousands of dollars on your home.

Inspector Gadget
Just like for an apartment, you will need to go through the home inspection phase. For houses, this is a bit more detailed and complicated. You have more serious issues to tackle, like the foundation, roof, construction, plumbing, heating/cooling systems, and electrical circuits of the house. You should consult with someone who is certified by the American Society of Home Inspectors. People with this certification will know exactly what to look for (like termites, faulty pipes, and toilets that don't flush) when inspecting the house. You should also be aware that most contracts usually allow between 1% and 2% of the purchase price for repairs to be made by the seller.

The Escrow Account: Purchasing a Home
Here's a general rule of life: nobody trusts anyone. It's unfortunate, but true. And that's why there's an escrow account. When an offer is finally made and accepted, the buyer is hesitant to hand over the money before getting the house, and the seller is hesitant to hand over the house before getting the money. So, once again, there's a third party—called the escrow agent—to be the middleman. This account is run by a financial institution, which is the mortgage company lending you the money. The way it works is that once you are ready to buy the house, you give your money to the escrow account. Think of it like Fort Knox. Once it goes in, it's going to need special permission—either you or your attorney's permission—before it comes out (unless you're a genius thief, in which case you can afford to pay for all this in cash). After the money is deposited into the escrow account, the seller knows you are serious about buying their house. It's only then that they hand over the paperwork, because once they do so, you are obligated to tell Fort Knox to give the seller their money.

The Escrow Account: Monthly Payments
In most states, once you submit your monthly mortgage payment, the mortgage company (lending institution) will take the portion of your mortgage that relates to real estate taxes, homeowner's insurance, and private mortgage insurance, and place them into an escrow account. The lender then disburses these funds on behalf of the borrower as the bills become due.

Types of Mortgages

While there are multiple variations of mortgages available, the very core of mortgages can be classified into two general categories: basic fixed and adjustable:

1. Basic Fixed: This mortgage represents a steady monthly payment of principal and interest for either 15 or 30 years. Each month, your payment is the same, and it remains steady until the entire mortgage is paid off.

2. Adjustable Rate Mortgage (ARM): This mortgage is a loan type that allows the lender to adjust the interest rate during the course of the loan (usually based on market and economic conditions with a predetermined cap limit).

Done Deal

When the offer is accepted, and all the negotiating nonsense is in the past, it is now time to sign the paperwork. At this point, you will also need a certified check to pay the monumental amount of money for the down payment and other associated costs. You will also need a box of tissues and possibly some smelling salts to help you actually *hand over* that check. It's a tough decision, but you knew this day would come. The paper signing ceremony is not as glorious as the one to sign the Declaration of Independence, so you don't need a fancy pen. But you will need one that has a lot of ink. Among the documents you will be signing and paying are:

- The sales contract
- Title/deed to the property
- Down payment
- Closing costs (legal fees, transfer fees, etc. Usually 1.5% - 4% of purchase price)
- Title insurance application (this is a closing cost to cover legal fees and expenses necessary to defend the title against claims made against ownership of a property)
- Settlement statement (document showing who has paid what to whom)
- Homeowner's insurance application

Check with your Title Company or realtor to determine if there are any other documents to sign. Don't worry if you don't know what most of these documents are, as your agent or attorney will gladly explain to you the importance of each one. Keep in mind that by this stage in the game, you will want to get out of there as quickly as possible. So just be patient, sign the paperwork, and move into your new home!

III. Move Out!

Congratulations! You're off to a new start, moving on to a new place, with lots of opportunity and challenges. Unfortunately for you, one of the biggest hurdles you'll encounter is the moving process. If you're going off to college, it might be nerve-racking, but at least you're not packing *all* your stuff (you're leaving your stuffed bunny from third grade behind). However, if you're making a permanent move—and therefore bringing Bunny along—fasten your seatbelts, because it will be a long ride. Most people don't know the right questions to ask, the appropriate actions to take before the move, or the things to look for in a moving company. The guide below will help you get through the stressful time, so you and Bunny can make the move fairly smoothly.

Move Over, Movers!
Hiring professional movers can be so expensive, you might be forced to eat 59-cent pasta for the next few years. (For those of you only eating the 59-cent pasta, please refer to the cooking chapter in this book. There are some tasty—and cheap—dishes listed there!) If you have the muscles of a body-builder, or simply ten good friends who are willing to help you move, you can move all your stuff in a budget-friendly way via self-moving companies.

The Self-Moving Industry
The way most self-moving companies work is that you pack all your belongings in boxes, and place them into a big truck (or pod). The company will then drive that pod/truck to your new home, and you once again unpack everything yourself. It is a lot of work, but if you're on a tight budget, you might be better off using a self-moving company (see company listings in Appendix A). Just think, with your monster savings, you'll be able to upgrade and buy the 79-cent pasta.

The Big Leagues
Assuming you've made the decision to ~~starve~~ hire professional movers, here is the basic checklist, concepts, and questions you'll need to ask before hiring your new muscle.

Questions to Ask Movers

Before you make a hasty decision on what mover to use, here are a few questions you should ask them *before* you sign any contracts.

1. How do you determine your estimate/bid? How much do you charge per hour?

2. What factors can change the price of my move? (Such real-life examples include delivering boxes to an elevator building or carrying items up several flights of stairs).

3. Do you have liability insurance? What kind? (Be careful on this one, because most movers only have coverage for a certain amount of cents per pound. That being the case, if your historic mocking bird feather costs $200,000, and it gets torn in the moving process, you'll have to pluck another bird.)

4. What types of damages are *not* covered under your insurance? (Brace yourself, their list WILL be long!)

5. Are there certain items your company will not move? (Do you think anyone would honestly move your razor-sharp pet porcupine with their bare hands?)

6. Will my stuff be on one truck the whole time? (Just think, if your contents are being shoved from one truck to another, your Aunt Bettie's fragile and priceless vase might not make it to its final destination in one piece.)

7. Is it a direct delivery, or will the truck stop somewhere else first?

8. Do you use subcontractors to move my stuff? If so, what are their names?

9. What kind of training do you give your movers for fragile items? (If there's a long pause or awkward hesitation on the other end, consider your stuff already broken.)

10. What services does this estimate/bid include? Is there

anything else you will do and charge extra for?

11. How long have you been in business? Can you please provide me with some current references/customers? (If they're most recent client is King Henry IV from 1399, you might want to ask if they've ever moved anything besides a throne.)

12. How much notice do you need before I commit to a final moving date? (Most movers need a few weeks notice. If you get a response like, "We'll be right over to pick up the stuff," hang up and immediately dial 911. You're being robbed.)

One Month Before You Move

1. Get Rid of Junk—Consider holding a garage sale or selling the items on eBay to get some cash for them. Of course, if you're trying to sell an old shirt with stains, the garbage might be willing to accept it.

2. Contact the IRS & Post Office for Change-of-Address Forms— These are critical documents because without the official changes, you'll be missing out on all your mail for a long time. And if you fail to contact the IRS and try to evade your taxes, you'll risk getting a new permanent address—the slammer.

3. Search for a Mover—Use the list in the Appendix or your local Yellow Pages to find a reliable mover, asking them all the questions outlined above.

4. Boxes Wanted—Time to start your search for boxes. Buying new boxes can be expensive, so here are alternative ways to obtain them. Go to your local grocery or wholesale market, and ask the manager if he has any extras available. Beware, however, that if you see a nice big box on the street corner, don't snatch it up—it could be a homeless person's house.

5. Medical Records—Get copies of your records from all your current doctors, and ask for referrals to new ones.

Two Weeks Before You Move

1. Cancellation of Services—Call all utility services and inform them of your move. This includes telephone service, water, electricity, and cable/magazine subscriptions. Instruct them to cancel your service the day *AFTER* you move. (Just think, if you cancel everything a few days before the big move, you'll be sitting in a dark room, with no food, water, furniture, electricity, TV, or phone. With a situation like that, you might as well pitch a tent on the street.)

2. Checking Accounts—Close any local checking accounts, and have your money transferred to your new bank. Naturally, if there is a branch of your current bank in your new hometown, you might not have as much work to do. Go into the bank and speak with a banking professional to see if there are any provisions for you to make.

3. Safe-Deposit Items—Collect all valuables, such as your birth certificate, jewelry, first tooth you lost, and anything else locked away in a safe-deposit box.

4. Check Itinerary—Call the airline or bus service you'll be taking to confirm your travel arrangements. You don't want moving day to come, and find out your flight has been cancelled with no replacement. If that were to happen, you'd finally understand the prior advice about not taking that big box on the street corner.

5. Start Packing—Put things into boxes, marking each box with black marker to help you identify what's inside when you get there. Things that are more important need special marking to help you recognize the most important stuff when you get to your new home. Be wise, and don't mark boxes with labels that will attract unwanted attention, such as "Ten Thousand in Unmarked Bills." Guaranteed you'll be mysteriously missing that box when you get there.

The Day of the Move

1. Double Check Everything!—There's nothing worse than leaving your favorite watch or hat in an empty drawer in your old home. One final time, go through your place, checking all empty drawers, closets, and chests for loose items.

2. Carry Important Documents—Don't let your important documents out of your sight. Carry them in a backpack or briefcase.

3. Money—Keep a sufficient amount of cash or traveler's checks on you, so you have easy access to it.

4. Important Numbers/Info—Keep a notebook of all critical phone numbers and contact information, such as family members, friends, and the address/phone number of your new home.

5. Keys—Be sure you have the keys to your new place before you leave your old one. Wouldn't it be a bummer to travel hundreds of miles to your new home, only to find that you're locked out, and the landlord is out of town? You might have to find another box on a street corner.

When You Arrive

1. Get a Phone Book/Maps—You might not be familiar with your new hometown, so gather all the local info you can, spotting the local stores, markets, and mud-wrestling bars (they really are popular in some cities).

2. Begin to Unpack—This may be emotional, especially if you're far away from friends and family. So do your best and don't overwhelm yourself by attempting to unpack everything on the first day. Unpack your most important items first (e.g. Bunny), and make it a step-by-step process. Here's where those specially marked boxes pay off.

3. Go Grocery Shopping—This will be one of the first things you

do, as most people need to eat! Stock up on a variety of foods, especially foods that don't require the use of a microwave, oven, or stove. You might not have access to them (or know how to use them!) for a day or two.

4. Introduce Yourself to the Neighbors—Be friendly and take a proactive approach to introducing yourself. Unless you live in a super friendly small town (like Little Heaven, Delaware), most neighbors won't be instantly bringing you housewarming gifts.

5. Car Info—After a day or two of settling in, take a trip down to the department of motor vehicles to get your new license, plates, registration, and auto insurance (if you don't already have it).

Chapter 4 Homework Reading—Recommended Books

Title: *The World's Easiest Pocket Guide to Renting Your First Apartment*
Authors: Larry Burkett, Ed Strauss
ISBN: 1881273962
Publisher: Moody Press

Title: *Decorating Your First Apartment: From Moving In to Making It Your Own*
Author: Paige Gilchrist
ISBN: 1579905137
Publisher: Sterling Publishing Company, Incorporated

Title: *Home Buying For Dummies*
Authors: Eric Tyson, Ray Brown
ISBN: 0764553313
Publisher: Wiley, John & Sons, Incorporated

Title: *Home Buyer's Checklist: Everything You Need to Know--but Forget to Ask--Before You Buy a Home*
Author: Robert Irwin
ISBN: 0071373802
Publisher: McGraw-Hill Companies, The

Title: *The Moving Survival Guide: All You Need to Know to Make Your Move Go Smoothly*
Author: Martha Poage
ISBN: 0762735740
Publisher: Globe Pequot Press

Chapter 4 Summary—The Least You Need to Know in Order to Pass the Class

1) Calculate how much you can afford before you start shopping for an apartment.

2) Search for apartments using word of mouth, classifieds, message boards, and simply driving around neighborhoods.

3) Inspect the premises using a checklist, taking note of the exterior, interior, general upkeep, and location of the apartment.

4) To buy a home, you will need to know how much you can afford for a down payment, as well as the monthly mortgage amounts.

5) Your real estate agent will assist you throughout the process of finding, buying, and closing on a home.

6) Use a moving checklist to ask the moving companies the critical questions, comparing them to competitors.

7) Have a designated schedule of what needs to be done before, during, and after your move. This includes transferring doctor records, canceling utilities, and getting your new driver's license in your new home.

CHAPTER 5—CARS:
Dude, Where's My Car?

"Car sickness is the feeling you get when the monthly payment is due."

—Author Unknown

Rev Your Engine

Finding a car today can be scary, intimidating, and expensive. There are essentially three ways to get a car (actually there are four, but don't count on hot-wiring it and making it onto the opening segment of *America's Most Wanted*). They include: buying used, buying new, and leasing. Hold onto your hats for this ride—you might be shocked to learn some of the tricks of the trade.

In this chapter, you will learn how to:

- Locate used cars in places other than dealerships

- Make sure the used car is in good condition

- Get the best deal on a new car

- Decipher the confusing language of auto insurance

- Decide whether you should lease or buy

I. Buying a Used Car

When you ask most people where to buy a car, they will tell you a dealership. Leasing or buying a car from a reputable dealership has its positives—but it can also leave a dent in your wallet. Before resorting to the classical methods of buying a car, learn from Lois Bidder, a local from Cheapside, Texas, and consider these other alternatives.

Buying a Car Online? Are You Nuts?

Nah, you're much smarter than the average person. Lois will be the first to tell you that you don't buy a car online the same way you buy a pair of socks. She bought a pair of socks online, believing the listing that they were "new." Unhappy when they arrived, she realized it was a scam. The socks came complete with a note that read, "The holes and nasty smell are 'new to you.'" If you are diligent with your research, and know how to weave through Internet traffic, you can land-cruise yourself a nice—and inexpensive—car. At www.ebaymotors.com, almost 450,000 cars were auctioned off last year alone! While market research is not conclusive, it appears to outsell holey and smelly socks 450:1.

Other Online Used Car Dealerships

There are multiple online used car dealerships to search. Lois Bidder really likes www.cars.com and www.carsdirect.com (full contact information is in the car appendix). These are very useful Web sites to browse, and gain an understanding of what is on the market. Be sure to compare apples to apples (e.g. same model number, year, model, and make) when you compare a car from one Web site to another. Lois thought she had found a spectacular deal on a car with a sun roof for half the price on one Web site compared to another. Little did she know they meant the roof was torn off in a train wreck, and it had a nice aerial view.

Newspaper Boy

The car you are looking for might be in your own backyard—literally. Lois Bidder opened up the classifieds section of the newspaper, looking for people who were selling used cars. She found a description of what she was looking for—and in the price range she was willing to spend. She gave the neighbor a call, asking how many miles it had, the year, model, and VIN number of the vehicle. She then checked the market value and continued with the research tips listed below. Lois was unfortunately misled, however, and thought that since it was such a friendly neighborhood, she could take the car for a test drive without the owner's permission. She should have realized she was doing something wrong when she used a crowbar as a key to unlock it.

Go to Jail—For a Day

After Lois was arrested for the crowbar incident, she was shocked to find out that jail was one of the best places to look for a cheap used car. It might sound crazy, but believe it or not, police stations sell cars. How, you ask? Well, it's simple. Cars get taken into police custody all the time, for a myriad of reasons. Murders, gang busts, drug deals gone awry, and the list goes on endlessly. But the important information is that cops take these cars, and once they're done processing them for evidence, they sell them to the public— sometimes directly and other times through an auction. Call your local police station and ask for more details. It can certainly be hit-or-miss (pun intended), but if you find a car that raises your eyebrows, continue with the research techniques listed below.

Salvage Auctions: Beware of the Rebuilt Wreck

A fact that most people are not aware of, is that cars that have been totaled are rebuilt. Totaled—as in completely demolished. Some salvage auctions will showcase a rebuilt car that has the appearance of looking fine on the outside—but is crummy on the inside. You might get lucky and find a car that's both nice on the outside and inside, but before you trust your smile from the shiny reflection of that red corvette, do some investigating.

True Colors

When you find the specific model and year you want, take that information and head over to sites like www.Edmunds.com or www.NADAguides.com (see a full listing in the car appendix) where you will find the true market value of the car. You can also use books such as the *Kelley Blue Book* and *Consumer Reports* to get these prices. The reason for doing this is to find out if it's a good deal from the get-go.

EXAMPLE: If you discover a car listed on eBay for $2,000, and then you find out that the true market value of the car is a mere $1,000, you know someone on the other end of the keyboard is trying to steal your money. On the other hand, if the market value is really $3,000, this is one car you want to examine more closely and continue to show interest in. Be wise and do your homework. It will pay off.

Safety Concerns

Not all cars are created equal. Some cars are safer than others. How so, you ask? Some larger cars have a higher chance of flipping over if you make a sharp turn. Other cars don't have the strongest exterior, allowing the car to fold like a tin can if it's in an accident. For a complete listing on safety and other important information, check out www.consumerreports.com, www.jdpower.com, www.safercar.gov, and the *Kelley Blue Book*.

I Found the Car of My Dreams—Now What?

If you are lucky enough to find a car that looks nice and is within budget, here's a step-by-step process to make sure you don't get stuck with a lemon.

1. **My Cousin VIN-ny**: Look for the sticker on the driver's-side doorjamb that shows the Vehicle Identification Number (VIN). Then compare that number to the VIN number on the dashboard. If it does not match, chances are this was a demolished car and the door has been replaced. This should raise a red flag to make you more cautious about proceeding forward.

2. **Do Your Homework:** Take the VIN number, and start your research. Go to Websites such as www.carfax.com or www.autocheck.com (see the car appendix for a full listing), where you can get background history on the car. The main areas of concern are if the car was in multiple auctions, has a long list of police reports, numerous transfers of title, and other important information (e.g. if someone tried to fraudulently change the odometer). If any of these items pop up, you might want to pop out. Expect to pay approximately $20 for this service.

3. **Body Wars:** If the car passes these initial tests, you're ready to take it to the body shop. Often confused with the popular Muscle Beach gym in sunny California, the body shop will help you search the vehicle for repainting and collision damage. Instruct them to do a full inspection, seeing if it has repair welds, salvage-yard repair parts, or was once the shape of an accordion. Having such an inspection generally costs between $25 and $125. Now that's a good workout.

4. **Start Your Engines:** If the car continues to look like it's in good shape, you're now ready to take it to Maury, the local mechanic. Have him check, double-check, and triple-check that the brakes work, the car drives straight (that's not a joke!), the fuel lines are not broken, the air bags are fully functional, and that parts haven't been replaced by those of inferior quality. This tune-up usually will run you between $50 and $125.

The "As Is" Concern

When buying a used car, be careful about contracts that say you are buying the car "As Is." These two words should be highlighted in yellow and raise immediate red flags. Instead, these two deadly words are usually buried among a bunch of other legal mumbo jumbo. Buying a car "As Is" means that once you leave with your new car, any problem—anything—is your problem. Read through the fine print and make sure the contract is free from an "As Is" clause.

Title Means It's Yours

No matter how much time, energy, and money you've invested in this car, it won't be legally yours unless the title is in your name. This is the most crucial document you have by the time you leave with the car. So, instead of your designated title (MD, JD, or CPA), make sure you get the one that really counts—the car title.

When You Drive Away. . .

You should have:

- The car title
- A signed copy of the bill of sale
- Repair or maintenance records
- Any special keys (e.g. for the gas tank, trunk, glove compartment, etc.)

You Just Never Know

It is also highly recommended that with your new purchase, you obtain an extended warranty, which can be bought from an array of online dealers. Additionally, you will need car insurance. Both of these topics are covered in detail in the new car section below, with full contact information in the car appendix.

To Save a Little Extra. . .

You might want to shop around for the cheapest gas prices in your area. You can make your job much easier by visiting www.GasBuddy.com and www.GasPriceWatch.com, which map out the cheapest gas prices all over the country!

II. Buying a Brand-Spankin'-New Car

Okay, Sparky, you apparently have some money to play with, and figure you'll go with a brand-new car. Maybe you're thinking SUV, Porsche, or a nice family car—like a tank. As you may have heard, buying a new car can be expensive, stressful, and daunting. There are hundreds of books, articles, Web sites, and other news-related information on the market. It's quite easy to get overwhelmed with information, so here it is broken down into bite-sized chunks. No matter how overwhelmed you may feel, take solace in the fact that Patrick Brane, the poor loser you will soon meet, got scammed on cars for his whole family before he finally got it right. To save space (and trees), his name will be abbreviated to P. Brane for the remainder of this section.

What To Do Before You Walk Into A Dealership

A word of caution before you embark on this journey. Dealerships are like playgrounds for grown kids. There is Bull, the big bully, and little Mikey, the skinny, pimple-faced kid who hopes his lunch doesn't get taken away. As you would expect, when Bull sees Mikey in the playground, he thinks it's his turf and can beat poor Mikey up. While not all car salesmen are bullies, many of them will think of the dealership as their playground—a place where they can push you around. So do your research and follow these steps, and you'll leave any dealership with a H.O.T. R.O.D. :

How Much You're Worth—Credit Checkup

Out-of-Pocket Expense—The Monetary Ballpark

Time of the Year to Buy

Remaining Payments—Financing the Sucker

Only Buy With a Warranty

Drive Away With Auto Insurance

Step #1: How Much You're Worth—Credit Checkup

Most people don't know what their credit score is, let alone try to improve it. As a high school—or even college—graduate, it's likely that you will not have any credit history. This is not necessarily a bad thing, just part of reality. Nonetheless, below is information on how and why you need to know your credit score, as it will become crucial later on in life.

Why It's So Important
Your credit score ultimately determines how much you'll be paying in interest when you finance your car. P. Brane had a poor credit score and the dealerships charged him astronomically high interest rates. Even worse, P. Brane didn't know his credit score and the dealership purposely tricked him into signing a finance program with a higher interest rate.

Where to Find It
There are several major national credit reporting agencies where you can go to obtain your credit report, which will include your credit score. The names, phone numbers, and Web sites for these companies can be found in the car appendix. You can get your credit report from any of these Web sites for approximately $10 (plus any taxes and shipping/handling fees.) When P. Brane finally heard this advice, he screamed out, "Ten dollars? That's more than I make per hour! I'd rather spend that money on dinner." The genius that he is, P. Brane got scammed into paying the astronomically high interest rate on his car, because he never knew what his credit score was. Way to go, P. Brane.

How to Read It
Your credit score is called FICO, which stands for Fair, Isaac, and Company, which is the company in California that developed the system. The score comes in three digit numbers, ranging from 300 (being the worst) to 900 (being the best), with the majority of people ranging between 600 and 700. The magic number is 680. If you have a credit score above 680, you'll be able to get a good rate on financing your car. If you're below 680, the odds are very much against you. And if you fall below 550, don't bother going to the dealership—they

most likely won't sell you a car. You can guess which category P. Brane fell into.

Step #2: Out-of-Pocket Expense—The Monetary Ballpark

When you have a general idea of what kind of car you want to purchase, go directly to the manufacturer's Web site and check out the cars and their options. There, you should be able to find the invoice amount, base amount, MSRP (Manufacturer's Suggested Retail Price), and local dealerships that sell them. Get an idea for what kind of monetary "ballpark" you're dealing with, and how much you can afford to spend. You can also get an average price by visiting multiple companies and Web sites, which are listed in the car appendix. You may also want to check out reports on different cars, such as those in "Car Review" and "Car & Driver," also available in the car appendix. Get a purchase quote from the Web sites, because you can use it as a negotiating tool at dealerships. P. Brane neglected to do any research, thinking he could instinctively feel his way through the negotiating process. When it was all over, the only thing P. Brane could feel was the emptiness in his wallet.

Step #3: Time of the Year to Buy

It's a known fact that the best time to buy a new car is the last two weeks of December and the months of July through October. You can still get good deals at other times of the year, but those times in particular are the prime season to shop. As you can probably guess, P. Brane was a Scrooge around the holiday season, and insisted the car dealership advertisements were a scam. For the first time, P. Brane was partially right—he got scammed out of a good deal.

Step #4: Remaining Payments—Financing the Sucker

P. Brane was disillusioned and thought he would soon inherit a large sum of money, and be able to pay for the car in one shot. When the time came to buy the car, and no rich relatives had died, P. Brane realized he would need to finance a large portion of the cost. He had to put a down-payment on the car, while the rest of the money was borrowed. P. Brane made monthly car payments until the loan was completely paid off. P. Brane mistakenly thought the dealership would be a Good Samaritan and lend him the money for free. Soon, he woke up from his dream, and realized they were charging him quite a high interest on that loaned money. They charged him interest—known as the Annual Percentage Rate (APR)—which was calculated primarily based on his credit score (discussed above). Do not be like P. Brane and wait until you get to the car dealership to start determining your financing options. Visit company Web sites, and get their contact information located in the car appendix. Auto loans are offered over the Internet. You can even get pre-approved with good credit but, of course, P. Brane didn't think of that.

How Long Should I Finance For?

Lenders will give you several options, usually anywhere between 1 and 6 years. Most people agree that you shouldn't borrow any longer than 4 years. The reasoning is simple: most warranties extend about 3 years, and you don't want to be stuck paying interest on a car that isn't even under warranty! So hunker down, and refuse the longer financing periods—it will help you in the long run.

WARNING: Beware of advertised rates that say an "introductory offer" or valid "for the first year." Many dealerships will try to hook you by advertising an extremely low interest rate—for the first year, then it skyrockets for the remainder of the loan. You want a rate that will be low and consistent throughout the life of the loan.

Step #5: Only Buy With a Warranty

As dense as P. Brane was, he knew he wasn't stupid. He knew that one of the most critical aspects of buying a new car is the warranty that comes with it. Most new cars will come with a standard manufacturer's warranty, and the dealerships will attempt to sell you an extended warranty. Each car manufacturer and dealership has different warranties, so there's no blanket rule about whether to get it or not. However, you can do a significant amount of research (and bargaining) by searching online for extended warranties. Such companies and Web sites can once again be found in the car appendix. They offer extended warranty deals that may be up to 50% less than the dealership will offer you. Get quotes and print them out. It's more ammunition you will need when going to the dealership. Regardless of whether you get an extended warranty or simply stick with the manufacturer's warranty, be sure to know exactly what the warranty covers—and what it doesn't. P. Brane felt good about himself when he got a warranty that covered everything on the car— the transmission, engine, radio, leather seats, and speedometer— until he realized that the warranty was only good for 30 days.

Step #6: Drive Away With Auto Insurance

P. Brane forgot that regardless of how he bought his car, he still needed auto insurance to go with it. Every state requires auto insurance if you're driving a car around town, so unless you plan on using a skateboard to get to work, this will apply to you. Naturally, P. Brane thought he was special (which he is, in many other ways) and didn't need auto insurance. Simply put, an auto insurance policy is a contract between you and the insurance company. You pay a designated amount (called a premium), and in return, the insurance company will pay for certain car-related financial losses during the time you are under contract with them. When you know which car you're interested in, call up all the insurance companies and get a quote, which is an estimate of how much you will pay in premiums. Auto insurance companies are also listed in the car appendix. This should go into your budget when calculating how much you can afford to spend per month on your car.

Say What?
Auto insurance terms can be confusing, so here are some brief definitions to help get you started.

Bodily Injury: P. Brane hit old lady Betty in her snazzy sports car, and she broke a nail. This coverage would have helped P. Brane pay for her injuries (consult your insurance company to see if manicures are covered).

Property Damage: P. Brane hit old lady Betty, and she lost control of her car, finally coming to a halt in someone's dining room. Property damage would have helped P. Brane pay for that broken dining room table (and other associated property expenses).

Personal Injury Protection: When P. Brane hit Betty, his mother-in-law was in his backseat and hurt her back. This coverage would have helped pay for any bodily damage to P. Brane and any passengers in his car (who will probably learn from their mistakes, and never trust him behind the wheel again).

Uninsured Motorist: Now reverse the situation, where old lady Betty hit P. Brane, and it was her fault. Poor Betty forgot to get auto insurance (which is illegal, but she's old, so give her a break). This coverage would have helped cover P. Brane's injuries when the other motorist did not have insurance.

Comprehensive: This would have helped pay for damage done to P. Brane's car when no accident occurred. Examples include natural disasters, theft, or a dead body landing on the car roof after being thrown from a 50-story building. (Don't you love that part in a movie?)

Summary

These steps are crucial to saving thousands of dollars when you buy a new car. Researching with these steps will take you weeks, maybe even months. However, once you gather your information and organize it, you can walk confidently into the dealership. You should have printed out:

- Purchase quotes from the manufacturer's Web site
- Your credit report (with your credit score)
- Your pre-approval forms and other financing opportunities
- Extended warranty quotes from the various Web sites
- Auto insurance quotes

The mere sight of all this organized paperwork will make big bully Bull's henchmen quiver. They will shake in their boots while letting out a deep sigh. You know why? Because they know you will not—and cannot—be scammed. You've done your research and are prepared for what they will throw at you. Some scam artists will do everything they can to add on more features. But, for the most part, you'll be way ahead of the pack. And even if you're not ahead of most others, you'll most certainly be ahead of P. Brane.

What To Do When You Get To The Dealership

A Clear View
Naturally, you will want to inspect the vehicle and take it for a test drive. Make sure if it's a new car that the MSRP number is on the window. If it's not there, don't even consider the car as a potential buy. Move on to one that has the sticker. Also, make sure that the VIN number exactly matches the door, hood, engine, dash-board, and any other places it's attached. Nonetheless, don't become neurotic like P. Brane and ask to see the interior of the gas tank and the bottom of the tail pipe, inspecting for any mismatched stickers.

The Negotiator
Just remember one thing: He was born a salesman. That means no matter how prepared you are, he will, by nature, try to sell you something you don't need. Being prepared with the aforementioned materials is a must, but despite all that, he will try to haggle further. That's why it's important to bring a friend or family member— someone good with verbal skills—to help you when the going gets tough. Plus, you'll have an advantage: two against one. Except in the case of P. Brane, who brought his cousin Lou Pole to help him with the process. Two morons against a salesman. You figure out who prevailed.

Put It in Writing
Anything the salesman promises, make him put it in writing. He might say, "I'll throw in three free oil changes," but when you get caught up in the moment, it's forgotten. Anything they promise—put it in writing. P. Brane forgot to get his free oil changes in writing, so when he came back and they denied him, he made a big fuss in the dealership. Finally, he was put in his place when the dealership manager said to him, "Who do you think the courts are going to believe—a reliable dealership that's been doing business for ten years or a guy named P. Brane?"

It All Adds Up

Dealerships will try to tack on extra fees. They will be relatively small charges here and there, but they add up. Some of these fees are legitimate and some are inflated. Be sure to discuss each and every "extra fee," challenging the salesman for its authenticity. There are so many extra fees floating around, it would be overwhelming and counterproductive to describe each in detail here. You can search for examples on the Internet, but at the end of the day, it's going to be your common sense and negotiating skills that help you reduce these add-ons. And you know where that left P. Brane—in a truckload of debt (and the truck he got wasn't worth it).

III. Leasing

Did You Say Lease or Leash?

Believe it or not, some people get the two words mixed up. Simply put, leasing means you are bound to a contract. You rent a car from a dealership, usually for lower monthly payments than if you were to buy the car and finance it. The selling price of the car is known as the Gross Cap Cost (or capitalized value). You can reduce the monthly payments by putting money down. You get to drive (and pay) for this car for the duration of your contract, and then return it at the end of the contract period. Think of it as a rental—only for longer periods of time.

The Eighth Wonder

The Eighth Wonder of the World is trying to figure out whether you should buy or lease a car. People are plagued every day with the struggle to decide. Based on much research and lengthy discussions with experts, the solution is simple: it depends on what you're looking for. Listed below are the positives and negatives of buying vs. leasing. Determine where your budget and mindset fit in, and the answer to what you should do will be crystal clear.

Will the Real Owe-ner Please Stand Up?

BUY: You are the sole owner of the car and get to keep it when you're through with your financing.

LEASE: You do not own the car. You are merely renting it and will have to return it when your contract is up.

Up Close & Personal

BUY: Up-front fees include: down payment + taxes + registration

LEASE: Up-front fees include: down payment + taxes + registration + first month's payment + refundable security deposit

The Monthly Payment

BUY: Higher payments because you're paying for the entire purchase price of the car.

LEASE: Lower payments because you're only paying for the depreciation of the car during the lease term.

The Mile High Club

BUY: You can drive as many miles as you want (but its value diminishes with higher miles).

LEASE: You are restricted to a limited number of miles during your lease term (usually around 15,000 miles).

When You Want a New Ride

BUY: You'll either have to trade in your old one or sell it.

LEASE: At the end of your lease, you can bring it in and get a newer model, or a new car, for a similar payment plan.

In Plain English

Here's the deal in plain, simple English. These are the bare-bone essentials of whether you should lease or buy.

If you:

- Want lower-overall monthly payments
- Like a new car every 2-3 years (that's under warranty)
- Are willing to pay a tad bit more over time in order to get these perks (higher long-term costs)

. . . you should **lease**!

If you:

- Want to ultimately own a vehicle with no monthly payments
- Are willing to pay the upkeep and maintenance costs (after the warranty)
- Prefer to pay higher initial monthly payments, but lower long-term costs

. . . you should **buy**!

Closing the Gap

One item that is of critical importance (if you lease) is gap insurance. As its name implies, gap insurance protects you from a scenario where your leased car is worth less than the amount you still owe on it.

EXAMPLE: If your leased car is worth $20,000, but you still owe $25,000 over the remaining course of the lease (because you're "leashed" to a contract!), then you might find yourself in some trouble if something happens to the car. If the car is totaled in an accident or is stolen, the insurance company will only reimburse you for the value of the car ($20,000). Yet you still owe $25,000 on the lease, leaving you with a hole in your pocket worth $5,000. That's where gap insurance comes in. It will help you close the gap between the value of the car and what you still owe to the dealership—so you won't be leashed to debt.

How to Play the Game

In some respects, leasing a car is entirely different from buying. But in other areas—such as the preparation and negotiating a deal—the two are like twins. Four out of the five steps outlined above in how to buy a car apply to leasing as well. In summary, here they are:

1) To find lease quotes, go to the companies listed in the car appendix and obtain price quotes. Print out these quotes and bring that sheet with you to the dealership so you can negotiate the deal.

2) Get your credit report from Equifax, Experian, or Transunion (all listed in the car appendix). Remember, your credit score will directly impact the monthly amount you'll be paying on the lease—and without knowing your own score, the dealership could pull the wool over your eyes.

3) In order to determine the financing for your monthly lease payments, use www.leasecompare.com. It will give you the flexibility to examine lease deals from several dealers. This way, you'll know the best financing deal even before you walk into the dealership.

4) Make sure you get your car insurance quotes before you go to the dealership, just as you would do if buying a new car.

5) Remember, there's no need to do research for a warranty (or an extended warranty) on a leased car because that's one of the advantages of leasing: it's under the warranty of the dealership! Any problems with it, and you bring it back!

In short, leasing and buying stem from the same family—but you have to do your homework. Do the research by finding online quote prices and financing, know your credit score, and investigate how much insurance will be. There's no substitute for being prepared with this arsenal of information.

Of course, as with any big purchase, before you fork over the money, ask advice from your family, friends, and peers. The people whom you trust the most are the best guidance. Older, wiser (although the two don't always go together), and more experienced folks know what to look for, so be sure to bounce your new find off them first.

Cars: Glossary of Terms

Acquisition Fee: Charged by the leasing party, sometimes amortized in the monthly payment and other times it's paid as an up-front fee. Consider this a fee for being "privileged" to rent the car from them.

Adjusted Capitalized Cost: The selling price, minus your down payment and any other rebates or trade-in values. This new adjusted amount is used to calculate your monthly payment.

Amortization: Paying off the debt of the principal and interest over a certain period of time. Think of it as a monthly paycheck – except your paying it instead of receiving it.

Annual Percentage Rate (APR): The annualized cost of credit expressed as a percentage. There is no annual percentage rate in a lease.

Bank Fee: Yet another one of those fees for the leasing company.

Base Monthly Payment: The portion of your monthly payment that relates to the depreciation of the car. This base amount + interest + tax equals your final monthly payment.

Base Price: The basic price of the car, not including any options or accessories. It only includes the basic manufacturer's warranty and standard equipment.

Credit Report: A summary of your financial situation, which contains your credit score. This has a direct impact on the type of loan you will receive to buy or lease a car.

Depreciation: The value that the car will lose during the course of the lease. Remember, it can't stay new forever!

Destination Fee: Moving the vehicle from the manufacturer to the dealer. The buyer pays this fee–but there should not be any extra inflated dealer's fee associated with it.

Disposition Fee: A fee the leasing company will charge you at the end of your lease to fix up the car for its new owner. (Man, they get you coming in, and then again going out!)

Down Payment: The amount of money you put down up front to help lower your monthly payments.

Early Termination Fee: An amount you will have to pay should you (gulp!) cancel your lease earlier than the contract states.

Excess Mileage Fee: The penalty the leasing company will charge you should you dare to go over the specified-miles limit.

Extended Warranty: This covers select problems you may have with the car after the manufacturer's warranty is up. You can purchase extended warranties from the manufacturer, the dealership, and other companies that can be found online.

Gap Insurance: This insurance will protect you in a situation where the value of your leased car is less than the remaining amount you owe on the lease.

Holdback: An allowance between 2-3% of the MSRP that manufacturers provide to dealers. It helps the dealer to pay the manufacturer less than the invoice price. That means a buyer could buy a car for less than the invoice price and the dealer would still make a profit!

Invoice Price (Dealer's Invoice): The amount the dealership pays for the car, which includes the destination fee (but remember, it actually costs them less than this).

Kelley Blue Book: A book that dealerships use to estimate the wholesale and retail value of a car.

Lease: A binding contract where the car dealer grants the customer the ability to drive a car in exchange for monthly payments.

Lessee: The person who signs the lease (that would be YOU!), indebting himself to pay the lessor for a certain amount of time.

Lessor: The person or dealership who grants you the lease. In layman terms, it's the bloodsucking dealership that tries to swindle the most money out of you. (An easy way to remember the role of each person is to consider the sounds of the last syllable when you pronounce "LessOR" and how strikingly similar it is to "OwnOR." The lessor is the true owner of the vehicle).

Monroney Sticker (see also Sticker Price): A sticker on the window of a car, showing the base price, the MSRP, and the destination charge. It's required by law for this sticker to be on each new car. If you don't see one, bust outta there like a bad habit.

Manufacturer's Suggested Retail Price (MSRP): Often times interchangeable with the Sticker Price. It's an inflated value that contains numerous options, accessories, and fees that can easily be negotiated down (and are purposely included so you feel good when you bargain them down).

Purchase Option Price: The selling price of your leased car at the end of your lease, should you want to buy it outright.

Rebate: The manufacturer's discount to buyers, so they will have an incentive to buy the car.

Residual Value: The estimated value of your leased car at the end of the lease term.

Security Deposit: Generally speaking, this is approximately one month of your lease payments, which the leasing company requires in case of excessive abuse or damage to the car. It is usually refundable at the end of the lease.

Sticker Price (see also Monroney Sticker): Generally, this is the MSRP price + dealer-installed options + dealer preparation + undercoating. You may hear people use the sticker price and MSRP price interchangeably, but sometimes the sticker price will include extra options and fees. Just remember, when you're buying a new car, you don't want to pay anything close to either the sticker or the MSRP price!

Termination Fee: A hefty charge you'll get nailed with if you cancel the lease before the end of your contract term.

Vehicle Identification Number (VIN): Think of it as the Social Security number of a car. It's a number that the manufacturer assigns to the car and is distinctive to each car. It also is written on the registration and title of the car.

Chapter 5 Homework Reading—Recommended Books

Title: *Buying a Car For Dummies*
Author: Deanna Sclar
ISBN: 0764550918
Publisher: Wiley, John & Sons, Incorporated

Title: *What Car Dealers Won't Tell You: The Insider's Guide to Buying and Leasing a New or Used Car*
Author: Bob Elliston
ISBN: 0452276888
Publisher: Penguin Group

Title: *Don't Get Taken Every Time: The Ultimate Guide to Buying or Leasing a Car in the Showroom or on the Internet*
Author: Remar Sutton
ISBN: 0141001496
Publisher: Penguin Group

Title: *Car Shopping Made Easy: Buying or Leasing, New or Used*
Author: Jerry Edgerton
ISBN: 0446672440
Publisher: Warner Books, Incorporated

Title: *AAA Auto Guide: Buying or Leasing a Car*
Authors: Jim MacPherson, American Automobile Association
ISBN: 1562515772
Publisher: AAA

Chapter 5 Summary—The Least You Need to Know in Order to Pass the Class

1) In addition to dealerships, search for used cars in other places, such as cars taken by the police, salvage auctions, newspaper, classifieds and online auctions.

2) Before buying a used car, take it to a mechanic and have him or her check the important components (such as the engine, brakes, fuel lines, etc.).

3) When buying a new car, know your credit score, the price you're willing to spend on the car, financing options, and warranties.

4) When buying a new car, do research on the rebates and holdbacks that come with the car, which will help you negotiate a lower price.

5) After learning the most important car insurance terminology, shop around for the best auto insurance deals.

6) Make an informed decision on whether to buy or lease based on your personal situation. Factors include whether you want a high or low monthly payment; like a new car every couple of years; and prefer to pay higher initial monthly payments, but lower long-term costs.

CHAPTER 6—MONEY:
Dollars & Sense

"The quickest way to double your money is to fold it over and put it back in your pocket."

—Frank Hubbard

Growing Pains

You probably know that money doesn't grow on trees, and you aren't as naïve as the guy who thought he could "grow" money by planting it in his flowerpot, adding a little water each day. The only thing you'll be growing is the deficit in your bank account. Some have more, some have less, but most people have to work hard for their cash. That's why this is one topic that should be a requirement in school. However, it isn't, so here's the rundown on everything you need to know, from simple bank terminology to the important basics of investing. So pay attention, because one of the biggest wake-up calls you get when you venture into the real world is that money matters.

In this chapter, you will learn how to:

- Write and deposit checks in the bank

- Understand the terms and verbiage of credit cards

- Make educated decisions about investing

- Create a realistic budget

- Choose a health insurance plan right for you

- Fill out the W-4 Form at work

I. Bank on It

The Bank

Banks are monetary institutions that you will come to love (or hate, if you are constantly asking them to loan you money). Banks have checking, savings, and CD accounts, which will all be explained below. Most banks have financial advisors who can recommend which account works best for you. These people can be helpful - but only after you know the basics of how things work. So take a lesson from Mr. E. Mann, who went to the bank mystified about financial institutions. Walking in wearing a cowboy hat, whiskers the size of licorice, and an old, dingy bag full of one-hundred-dollar bills, Mr. E. Mann met with Robin Banks, the advisor who taught him everything he needed to know.

Types of Accounts

To stay organized, many people use both a checking and savings account. "What's the difference?" Mr. E. Mann asked. In response to his question, Robin explained:

1. **Checking**: "You see, Mr. E. Mann, this type of account allows you to keep money in the bank while having the option to write checks. Some businesses (although they are few) will not take credit cards, and carrying large sums of cash is often inconvenient. Additionally, if your second-cousin's niece is celebrating her pet whale's ninth birthday, and you want to send money, best to do it with a check, not cash, for financial safety reasons."

2. **Savings**: "As its name implies, this account is used for saving purposes, and with this account, you rarely have the option to write checks from it. Certainly, if someone writes a check to you, you can bring it to the bank, and deposit it into your savings account. To encourage savings, Mr. E. Mann, our bank offers a higher interest rate than on a checking account." Leaning closer, Robin Banks whispers, "Although, between us, it's not much higher."

Better Than Under Your Mattress

Still unconvinced he should give his bag of money to Robin

Banks, Mr. E. Mann slouched back, propping his feet on Robin's desk. Mr. E. Mann questioned, "What happens if I give you my entire life savings, and you lose it?"

Not flinching, Robin Banks responded, "The most important aspect to picking your bank is to make sure they are FDIC insured. FDIC stands for the Federal Deposit Insurance Corporation. Having your money in a bank that is FDIC insured means that a force field is protecting it in case of an emergency. Up to $100,000 (per person) of your money is insured. That means that if, for whatever reason, our bank goes out of business, the federal government will make sure that you get your money back, up to $100,000."

Sparked by this phenomenon, Mr. E. Mann sat upright, asking, "So, if wild bandits robbed this place clean, taking even the socks off your feet, I'd still get my money?"

"Up to $100,000," Robin responded.

"Then why would I leave it under my mattress?" asked Mr. E. Mann.

"You wouldn't," Robin quipped.

Checks and Balances

After opening a checking and savings account with the bank, Mr. E. Mann held his new checkbook in his hand, not knowing what to do with it. "Are these vouchers good at the dog track?" Mr. E. Mann asked.

"Not quite," Robin responded. "You see, according to the textbook definition, a check 'is a written order to a bank to pay the amount specified from funds on deposit.' In plain English, it's a small slip of paper that can be redeemed for cash. If you are the recipient of the check, the payor will write your name, date, and amount in the appropriate boxes, and then sign it. The person who receives the check then takes it to their bank, and can either place it into their bank account or redeem it for cash. Think of it like the tickets you win from ski-ball, and then get to redeem them for the fake spider."

Mr. E. Mann replied, "But I hate spiders, and so does my wife. She makes me kill them every time one builds a web in her pantry. What if I wanted to buy another pet, one who could eat these little critters? How could I use these vouchers to buy one?"

Robin Banks realized this was going to take some teaching effort on her part. So she outlined the following tips for Mr. E. Mann:

When You're the Payor (Giver):

1. Keep a Log—Every checkbook comes with a separate little book with a bunch of blank lines, called a Check Register. These lines are to be filled in every time activity happens in your account. You start with your beginning balance (the amount you initially deposited in the bank), and you subtract any checks written and, of course, add any deposits you make into the account.

2. Learn to Spell Correctly—When you write a check, write the amount in numbers as well as words. As an example, if you write a check for two hundred dollars and fifty cents, you fill in **"$200.50"** in the box on the right hand side and **"Two hundred dollars and 50/100"** on the line in the center of the check. The words are essentially more important than the numbers, since if some of the numbers are smudged or are different from the words, the law states that the wording is used. The moral? Pay attention in English class.

3. Minimum Balance—Some banks will require you to have a minimum amount of money in your account at all times. If you are writing a check, be sure that the amount won't drop you below your minimum balance, or else the bank may charge you additional fees.

4. Everyone Makes Mistakes—If you are in the middle of writing a check, and accidentally make an error (and want to start over again), be sure to write in big capital letters across the front of the check: "VOID." This will assure that nobody can find that check in the trash and somehow present it to the bank and cash it.

5. Up Close and Personal—If you are writing a check in a store, be aware that they may ask you for some form of identification, such as your license or passport.

6. No Blank Spaces—Although not a law, it is highly recommended that you don't leave any blank space in the boxes where you fill in the amount of money you are paying.

Leaving any open space just gives more leeway for a crook to add on a word (or number), turning your $10 check into $100,000. No need to write big or use a thick marker. Just draw a line through any open space you are not using. This will deter criminals from altering your checks.

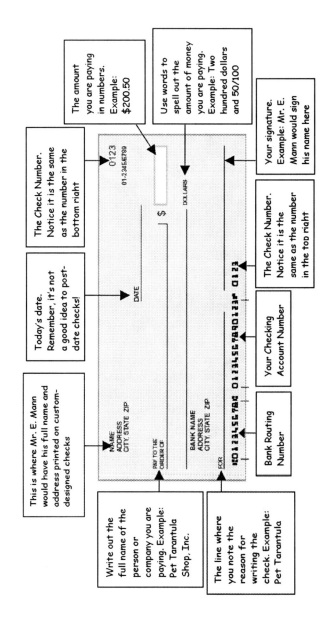

The amount you are paying in numbers. Example: $200.50

Use words to spell out the amount of money you are paying. Example: Two hundred dollars and 50/100

The *Check Number*. Notice it is the same as the number in the bottom right

Your signature. Example: Mr. E. Mann would sign his name here

Today's date. Remember, it's not a good idea to post-date checks!

The *Check Number*. Notice it is the same as the number in the top right

This is where Mr. E. Mann would have his full name and address printed on custom-designed checks

Your Checking Account Number

Bank Routing Number

Write out the full name of the person or company you are paying. Example: Pet Tarantula Shop, Inc.

The line where you note the reason for writing the check. Example: Pet Tarantula

When You're the Payee (Receiver):

1. The Back Side—On the back of the check, sign right next to the little "x" on the top. The action of signing a check is called endorsing the check. There are three types of endorsement on a check, but the ones most commonly used are the first two:

    a. Blank Endorsement—If Mr. E. Mann were to receive a check, he would merely sign the back of it with his legal name: "**Mr. E. Mann**." By signing this check, he is now allowing anyone who takes this check to the bank to cash it. This means that if he signs it, and then loses it, the finder can take it to the bank and cash it. (**Note:** Mr. E. Mann's birth certificate read "Mr. E. Mann" and he therefore had to sign his name in exactly that fashion. Had his parents been normal and merely called him "E. Mann," he would be able to sign his name without the "Mr." in front of it.)

    b. Special/Full Endorsement—This is used when a person receives a check, and wants to transfer it over to another party. Let's say Mr. E. Mann owes money to the exterminator for pumping his house full of toxic fumes to get rid of the spiders. If Mr. E. Mann gets a check in the mail for $150 from his work, and that is the exact amount of money he owes the exterminator, Mr. E. Mann can transfer the check over to the exterminator by writing the following on the back of the check: "**Pay to the order of Mr. Bug Killer**" and then he signs right underneath it, "**Mr. E. Mann**," showing that he is endorsing the transfer of this money.

    c. Restrictive Endorsement—This is when you want to be extra careful, and make sure that the check can only be deposited into your account, not cashed. Mr. E. Mann would write on the back of the check: "**For Deposit Only: Bank Account #12345678**" and then sign right underneath it, "**Mr. E. Mann**." The advantage of this safer endorsement is that if Mr. E. Mann lost the check, the finder would not be able to take it to the bank and cash it.

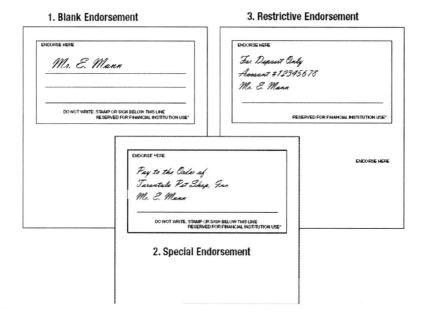

1. Blank Endorsement

3. Restrictive Endorsement

2. Special Endorsement

2. Cash Out Now!—A check legally becomes invalid a certain number of days after the date written on it. Each state has its own regulations, but it can be as short as 60 days, while some states will honor a check that is even a year old. So, if someone gives you a check, don't delay in taking it to the bank. The last thing you want to do is show up at the bank months later and have them say, "Sorry, you waited too long, and this check is no longer valid."

II. Credit Cards

The Basics
A credit card is a small plastic card, around 3 by 2 inches, that contains identification information such as a signature and series of 16 sequentially unique numbers. This card also has a magnetic strip on the back that identifies which account is being used. The person whose name is on this card will be sent a bill every month, showing the charges and transactions.

Meet Your Financial Enemy or Friend—It's Up to You
A credit card can be your financial enemy if you misuse it. On the other hand, if you pay off every bill on time and use it responsibly (sorry, until you can afford it, your pet whale goes hungry), it can build you a great credit rating. Meet Jack Pott, who went through the ups and downs of the credit card blues.

The Minimum "Deadly" Payment
Here's where Jack got into trouble. He got his bill at the end of the month for a total of $500, but the credit card bill had an option to pay the "minimum payment," (called the minimum "deadly" payment from now on). It was very small in comparison to the whole bill. It was only $25, and quite enticing indeed. Although he had $550 in the bank, Jack had the urge to attend a friendly poker game that night, and needed fast cash. So he decided to pay the minimum "deadly" payment, leaving enough cash left over for his late-night activities. Each month, Jack paid the minimum "deadly" payment, until a few years later, his minimum "deadly" payment was in the thousands! What Jack didn't realize was that this is how credit card companies stay in business.

Advice
Here's some advice regarding these minimum "deadly" payments: **DON'T DO IT!** The reason the credit card companies want you to make only the minimum payment is because they will charge you interest, up to a whopping 23%, every month if you become delinquent in your payments! The underlying principle is that if you don't make your payments on time, you'll be paying enormous amounts of money in interest. If you're not careful, over time, you can drown in credit card debt. The emotionless credit card jerks will

happily watch you squirm in the water—never throwing you a life preserver.

The Fringe Benefits
To make matters worse, Jack Pott's credit card didn't have any benefits. He thought he had to pay an annual fee in order to get rewards on it. True, there are credit cards on the market that charge an annual fee, but there are also plenty that don't—yet they have free (Free? Did someone say free?) rewards! Some have rewards in the form of airline miles, gift certificates to selected stores, and even cash back. These rewards are based on how much money you spend on the card, and are typically 1% in value of your total activity. You won't get rich from these rewards (duh), but they add an extra incentive to the convenience of paying with plastic. Jack was really disappointed to learn that his friends wouldn't accept a credit card to pay for his losses.

The Credit Card Mumbo Jumbo
Before you get plastic happy and go from store to store, frolicking with your shiny new credit card, pay attention to the legal credit card jargon. Spend wisely and frolic safely. So, before you C.H.A.R.G.E. it, make sure you known the terms.

Credit Line—Each card you have will carry an amount limit. That means you will not be able to charge more than that amount in any given month before paying off the bill. As an example, if Jack Pott has a $2,000 credit limit on his card, he will not be able to spend more than $2,000. Once he pays off that bill, his credit line starts over again. If you have good credit and make your payments on time, your credit card company will gladly raise your credit limit in increments over time. Just think of how many poker games Jack can attend if he has a high credit line.

Handouts (Called a "Cash Advance")—You will be offered the option to borrow a large sum of cash without paying for it—for now. However, if you are late in paying it back, they come after you with a pitchfork and electric chain saw. Okay, kidding—but not by much. When Jack Pott was charged such astronomically high interest rates, he began wishing they would come at him with that pitchfork and saw.

Annual Fee—This is a flat annual charge, very similar to what you would pay to belong to a local club or organization. Plenty of credit cards have no annual fee, so if you are paying an annual fee, have a good reason.

Rate (Annual Percentage Rate & Finance Charge)—Face it, nobody is going to lend you money for free (unless it's your parents, and even they are stingy these days). If you decide to borrow money from the credit card company (and don't pay it back in the next bill), you will be charged a very high interest percentage for the "privilege" of borrowing their money. This charge is known as the Finance Charge, and is calculated by annual percentage rate (APR). These interest rates can extend up to 23%. (You read correctly; there's no decimal in between the 2 and the 3.) The higher the APR, the more credit card debt you can get into. Superman has Kryptonite and humans have credit cards with high interest rates. It's that simple.

Grace Period—For people who make their payments on time, the credit card companies will usually give you about 25 days—your grace period—to make your payment without incurring any finance charges. Generous of them, don't you think?

Entry (Introductory) rate—Credit card companies love to attract you by slyly drawing you in with a lower APR rate for a short period of time. After that time period elapses, the interest will skyrocket faster than a new Ferrari. There's a word for companies like that: Bloodsuckers.

Conclusion

The best advice about credit cards is to keep track of what you're spending and realize it is just another form of payment. Most people don't keep a record of how much they put on their card, and worse yet, think of it as their personal lending warehouse (and all this time, you thought your Uncle Bert was really rich). The trick behind credit cards is to view them exactly as cash. Whatever amount of cash you have in your bank account is how much you can spend. If you use credit cards wisely, they can offer rewards (keep thinking that 1%, baby!), be a great convenience, and add value to your credit rating. If you use them improperly, you'll wind up like Jack Pott—and your winnings won't mean jack.

III. Investing

Five Critical Components

Investments are like octopi—they have multiple legs and are difficult to grasp. However, there are five basic criteria you should clarify when investigating a certain investment. Addressing these issues will make you aware of the investment's ramifications. Just remember, you are investing your time and M.O.N.E.Y.—something everyone wants to hang on to.

Make Sure It's Affordable—Someone might inform you of an awesome, can't-miss investment opportunity. But then you find out you need to fork out $50,000 in cash. If you can afford that, go for it! But if there's a chance you'll be sharing a box with the man on the street corner, find a cheaper investment. You should never—repeat, never—invest money that, if lost, will leave you broke.

Overall Diversification—If someone recommended that you eat ribs for breakfast, lunch, and dinner your entire life, you'd think they were crazy. In order to have a balanced "investment diet," you want to consume a diverse variety, making sure you receive the fringe benefits from all four food groups. Any Investing 101 course will tell you that your portfolio of investments should be diverse and spread out—among CDs, stocks, bonds, real estate, and retirement funds. Invest the way you eat—unless you're eating cows at every meal.

Name the Risk vs. Return—Every investment has a risk and return. The risk is the possibility of losing your money, while the return is the income earned on your initial investment. This return is usually determined as a percentage of your initial investment. As logic would dictate, the riskier the investment, the higher the return. Before throwing your money into an investment account, you should understand how risky it is and what type of return you can expect to see from it.

Early Escape: How Liquid Is It?—Until this point in your life, you've probably thought of liquid as a science term, along with solids and gases. But the financial world has its own definition of liquid: an investment that can easily be converted into cash. When you place your money in certain investments, it's like placing them in a time-coded vault that you can't open for a certain period of time. Certain long-term CDs and bonds require several-year commitments, which means you won't be able to access that money for a while. If your investment is not liquid, and you suddenly need a large sum of cash, you are going to be in trouble. Find out the liquidity of your investment, as it will help you determine if it's right for your situation.

Year-End Tax Effect—Just when you're having a great time in the investment playground, the government, also known as Uncle Sam, is the bully who will ruin it. Most, but not all investments are taxable. That means that even if you're earning a great return on your investment, the tax ramifications can be costly. It is therefore imperative to ask how each investment is taxed, and if the big bully will be stealing your lunch and dinner money. Heck, if he's feeling especially ruthless, he'll take your breakfast money too.

Overview of Investments

Investing and financial planning can be a very complicated world. In your quest through life, you will probably need the assistance of an accountant (preferably a CPA: Certified Public Accountant) and financial planner (preferably a CFP: Certified Financial Planner). All too often, people in the working world simply give their savings to their financial planners without ever knowing what the planners are doing with their money! To help you understand what your financial advisor will be doing with your money, here's a brief description of the major types of investments and financial instruments available. You might not be instantly rich, but with time, you will strike G.O.L.D.:

Get Certificates of Deposit (CD)

Opportunities Are in Stocks

Long-Term Is for Bonds

Diversify With Mutual Funds

Newlyweds

You're about to follow the financial disputes of Elle and Richard Cuss, a young, newly married couple, who have conflicting financial goals. Richard always wants to save, constantly looking for the best manner to grow their money. His name will therefore be abbreviated to Rich for the remainder of this story. Elle, on the other hand, is always asking to pamper their pet skunk, Stinky. She doesn't care if they go into debt in order to allow their pride and joy to live lavishly. Look closely at her full name. Elle Cuss can be rearranged to read "clueless." Since she really is clueless when it comes to financial matters, she'll be called that for the remainder of the story. Follow along, eager ones, because the story of Rich and Clueless is an amusing one.

Get Certificates of Deposit (CD)

Compact in Other Ways

No, a CD is not a Compact Disk as Clueless thought, although that's what she wanted to buy when she first heard the term CD. When Rich explained to her that CD stands for Certificate of Deposit, he elaborated, "CDs are one of the most conservative and safe investments available on the market. Like a bank account, they are insured up to $100,000 each (per person), and offer some attractive interest rates." It didn't help matters when the reply from Clueless was, "But Stinky's music CDs are also an investment—they help him meditate before he goes to sleep at night."

CDs in Action

"Okay," Clueless conceded, "you've piqued my interest in CDs. But how much money do we need to put into them?"

Surprised by her enthusiasm, Rich explained, "The way a CD works is that we invest a certain amount of principal money, as little as a few thousand dollars, for a designated period of time with a fixed rate of interest. These time periods can be as short as three months, and as long as five years. As logic would dictate, the longer the CD, the higher our interest. The only catch is that we can't take out our principal money during that time period, or else we'll get nailed with a steep penalty fee."

"But what if our little Stinky suddenly needs a new manicure and we need quick cash?" Clueless asked.

"That's why we won't put all our money in CDs. We'll only invest a certain percentage, leaving enough cash in our bank accounts in case of an emergency," Rich responded.

Proving the age-old theory that opposites attract, Clueless asked, "An emergency? Like Stinky needing a sponge bath in the summertime?"

The Bottom Line

"I'm starting to get confused," Clueless whined. "What's the bottom line of CDs?"

"A CD is one of the most conservative and less risky investments. It's a guaranteed amount of interest, and we're sure to walk away on top, assuming we keep our money in the account for the designated time period," Rich responded.

"Yay! So we're going to be rich! Let's put all our savings into CDs," Clueless exclaimed.

"Hold your horses, dear. Making rash decisions like that can only get us into trouble. And we don't want Stinky to get a heat rash now, do we?"

Opportunities Are in Stocks

Me? An Owner?

"Richy, CDs sound so conservative, and I don't think we'll become rich from them. Is there anything else out there?"

"As a matter of fact, there is," Rich replied. "It's called the stock market."

"Is that where we go to the market and stock up on Stinky's toiletries?" asked Clueless.

"No, not quite. If we buy stock in a public company, we are part owners of that company. That's what it means to own stock in them."

"Now that I'm a part owner, does that mean I can fire the booger-eating security guard in the front lobby?" Clueless asked.

"We don't get any hiring or firing rights, but we do get a piece of the action. We get to share in the profits and vote for the board of directors. Hundreds of thousands of public companies are traded on the stock exchange every day, and when we buy any amount of shares in the company, we are then "betting" on that company. In a simple analogy, think of it as going to a dog racetrack, and you place a bet on a dog to win. If it does well, you make money. If it tanks, well, then you lose money. In the stock market, however, you can bet on multiple "dogs" at the same time—and you can research more information on them than you could ever imagine." Rich explained.

"So, if we win big, I can buy Stinky his own massage hot tub!" Clueless said excitedly.

Rich could only groan and rub his temples in irritation.

No Jail Time for You
Even if you are part owner of a company, you have a limited amount of liability. If the company crumbles, and there are many lawsuits pending against the company, nobody will ever be able to come after you—as the stockholder. Clueless owned stock in a company that was later discovered to be committing serious fraud. However, just owning a piece of stock wasn't enough to incriminate her. The worst that happened to Clueless was that her stock in the company became worthless, and she lost her initial investment. That doesn't sound good, but when the company folded up shop, the real owners had a lot more grief to deal with than the stockholders.

The Big Picture
Clueless picked up a copy of the newspaper, quickly turning to the financial section. After about ten seconds, she ripped the newspaper in half, throwing it on the floor. Realizing Clueless was drowning in her lack of understanding, Rich decided to give Clueless a brief overview on how the market works.

The Stock Exchange: The Financial Store
Rich and Clueless went into the wild to find a pet skunk, but to no avail. All the candidates were either too immature, undeveloped, or not smelly enough. They finally went to a pet store, where they instantly fell in love with the most lethal-smelling skunk on the market—their cherished Stinky. Public companies that make their stock available for people to buy/sell can't do it in the "wild"—they need a meeting place, like a store. This place is called a stock exchange, and it is where stocks, bonds, and other securities are bought and sold. In the United States, there are numerous stock exchanges, including NYSE, NASDAQ, American Stock Exchange,

National Stock Exchange, and the Boston Stock Exchange, to name a few. The two largest stock exchanges are the New York Stock Exchange and NASDAQ. When a company becomes public, they get to choose which "store" they want to be in—but they can only choose one. Activity on these two exchanges is usually considered an indication of the state of the economy as a whole. Here's a little description of each:

1. **New York Stock Exchange (NYSE)**—This is physically located in New York City, where you see images on TV of stressed-out people waving their hands and screaming. (Maybe Stinky popped in for a while.) It's a private company owned by a bunch of shareholders, and usually trades companies that are well established and stable. The NYSE is an auction market, which means that when individuals are buying/selling, there is an auction occurring.

2. **National Association of Securities Dealers Automated Quotation (NASDAQ)**—The NASDAQ does not have a physical location. Rather, it is a sophisticated electronic network where investors make trades with buyers/ sellers. NASDAQ is a public company unto itself, which means that it has a lot more rules and regulations to follow. The companies that are traded on NASDAQ are usually more volatile, risky, and growth-oriented, like technology and Internet start-up companies. It is also a dealer's market, which means people are not buying/selling directly to one another, but rather are going through a dealer (called a market maker), who acts as a matchmaker between the two.

Comparison Between NYSE & NASDAQ				
	Location	Ownership	Overall Types of Companies Traded	The Manner in Which It's Traded
NYSE	Physically in NYC	Public	Well-established, blue-chip companies	Auction Market
NASDAQ	Electronic network	Private	High-tech, growth, and volatile markets (e.g. Internet, technology, etc.)	Dealer's Market

What Do You "Prefer"

There are two types of stock within each company. However, there is only one major difference:

1. Common Stock—This is the type of stock that most people have. It includes sharing in the profits of the company as well as voting for the board of directors.

2. Preferred Stock—While this type of stock has fewer rights than common stock, the main advantage of preferred stock is that the holders have first dibs on the dividends (profits) the company gives out. That means that if there isn't enough to go around, the people with preferred stock will get it first, and the people with common stock will get left behind.

Liquid Money

The nice thing about buying stocks is that you can buy or sell your shares any day the stock market is open (which is the five business/working days each week). There is no minimum or maximum time you have to hold onto a stock, so unlike bonds or CDs, you can buy today and sell tomorrow. This is good news for the newlyweds, who need their money available to buy air freshener when Stinky gets severe indigestion.

Dividends—Reward Money!

If you were fortunate enough to make it to the top of the food chain, wouldn't you want to reward the people who helped you get there? Well, maybe Clueless wouldn't but, thankfully, not everyone is like her. That's where dividends come in. Dividends are declared by a company's board of directors and are given to its shareholders out of the company's profits. Think of it as the company saying, "Thank you for investing in us and we want to express our appreciation by giving you a bonus." Dividends are usually given as cash (cash dividend), but they can also take the form of stock (stock dividends). Dividends provide an incentive to own stock in stable companies even if they are not experiencing much growth. Companies are not required to pay dividends, but those that do are most often companies that have progressed beyond the growth phase, and no longer benefit sufficiently by reinvesting their profits, so they usually choose to pay them out to their shareholders.

Types of Stocks: Large Cap, Mid Cap, and Small Cap

Like most things in life, you can get a small, medium, or large. There are three general categories a company's stock falls into. Large Cap Stocks are for large companies that have proven themselves in the past and are for the long-term investor. They pay high dividends. Mid Cap Stocks are companies that are still growing and are off to a great start but are still not in the same league as the larger companies. They don't pay good dividends because they use that "extra money" to fund their business. Small Cap Stocks are companies that are just starting, and although they might have a great service or product, they are unproven and quite risky. As you can imagine, Small Cap Stock companies rarely pay any dividends.

Stock Market Index: Stocks With Commonalities

"There are so many stocks, which ones should I choose?" Clueless cried.

"Nobody knows the definitive answer, Clueless, but there's something called an index."

"Like in the back of Stinky's *101 Ways to Make your Odor Fouler* book?" Clueless asked.

"Sort of. A stock market index represents the characteristics of its component stocks, all of which bear some commonality. They can include trading on the same stock market exchange, belonging to the same industry, or having similar market capitalizations. In fact, many indexes are used to judge the performance of portfolios such as mutual funds (which you'll learn about very shortly)."

"Wow! So someone has already done the hard work and organized the gazillion stocks into separate categories?" Clueless asked.

"Yes, although there are many, the most common indexes are: Dow Jones, Standard & Poors 500 (S&P 500), and Russell," Rich answered.

"What are we waiting for? Let's go look for. . ." Suddenly, Clueless fell to the floor, gasping for air.

"What is it, Clueless? Is this too much excitement for you?" Rich asked.

"No. . . it's Stinky. . . he just learned to read his book. . ." And with that, she fainted.

Legal Gambling

That's how Rich told Clueless to view the stock market—as a legalized form of gambling. Rich explained that this is because nobody *really* knows if a stock is going to go up or down. Analysts make educated guesses and try to study the statistics and nature of the market. But ultimately, there is no crystal ball that reveals what the future holds. Clueless therefore realized that buying stocks is considered one of the more risky investments. Rich insisted that part of their portfolio should consist of stocks—but he also warned that it could go up or down at any moment. For more information on purchasing stocks, see Appendix C with full contact information.

Long-Term Is for Bonds

An IOU Note

"Do bonds have anything to do with those ridiculous James Bond movies? Those loud noises scare me," Clueless said.

"No, Clueless, far from it. A bond is an IOU note given to us by an institution in exchange for money. The institution is going to pay interest—as a reward—for loaning them money for a specified period of time. Bonds are considered more conservative in nature, although they do have some risky aspects to them. The institution owes us, as bondholders, the original principal investment plus any interest agreed upon."

"Are these interest rates any better than the CDs?" Clueless asked.

"In fact, they may be slightly higher than CD rates," Rich explained.

"Great! Stinky can have three sponge baths instead of one!" Clueless declared.

Why Would Any Institution Do This?

Because they need the money. Institutions are no different than any of us. They have troubling times (but no, Stinky missing his bath is not considered a troubling time) and are often in need of money to continue operating their business. Borrowing money from outside sources—and giving an IOU note (the bond) in return—helps to keep the institution afloat.

Right Off the Charts

"But how will I know which bonds to invest in? There are hundreds—no, thousands—to choose from!" Clueless was worried.

"There's no need to panic, Clueless. Just like there's a ranking of your favorite pop artists on the weekly Top 40, there's also a rating system that exists for bonds. A bond is considered extremely safe, usually because the institution issuing it is doing quite well, and it will therefore receive the rating of AAA. The next best rating is AA, then A, and then it starts with BBB. This rating continues all the way through C," Rich explained.

"So why would anybody choose a bond with a low rating?" Clueless asked.

"Because the bonds with the highest ratings will usually have a lower return than the other bonds. Just remember, Clueless, the safer the investment, the lower the return. And the opposite is true as well: the riskier the investment, the higher the return."

Dazed and Confused

"But there are so many kinds of bonds out there, Richy. I still feel very overwhelmed," Clueless complained.

"Well, there are three basic categories of bonds: Treasury, Municipal, and Corporate bonds. Think of them like your closet of shoes. You have three categories of shoes for formal, casual, and sporty occasions."

"Richy! There are more occasions than that!" Clueless said, on the defensive.

"Let's pretend and say only three," Rich pleaded.

In Government We Trust—Treasury Bonds (The Safest)

While companies can always go bankrupt (and you can lose your investment), government bonds—often called US Treasury Bills (T-Bills)—are often considered a safer investment. The government has never failed to pay on its bonds, and while it's always a possibility that the government would not be able to pay you back, your money is in safe hands with the government.

State, City, and Other Local Bonds—Municipal Bonds (Still Very Safe)

Municipal bonds are backed by the state or city—whoever is issuing them. These bonds are used for projects to benefit the welfare of the community. (Sorry, Clueless, buying Stinky a new diamond necklace doesn't meet the criteria.) These projects can include building new roads, hospitals, and other local happenings in your state. The advantage of municipal bonds is that they are tax free—which means that when you receive your principal plus interest back from the city or state, you will not be taxed on it. Municipal bonds are slightly more risky than Treasury Bonds, as there have been cases (although they are very rare) where the city has gone bankrupt, and your investment goes up in smoke.

Corporate Bonds (Risky)

The final, and most risky, type of bond is a corporate bond. It should be no surprise (although to Clueless, everything is surprising) that companies need money just as much as the government does. The only difference is that companies go in and out of business all the time. Filing bankruptcy is a regular occurrence in corporate America. (Ever hear of Enron?) It is for that reason that corporate bonds are more risky than Treasury or Municipal bonds. Nonetheless, they usually have a higher rate of return, handsomely compensating the investor for the risk they have incurred. For corporate bonds more so than any others, it is critical to do the research and find out the bonds' ratings before you invest in them. Corporate bonds can be as risky as standing in the pathway of Stinky after he's had beans for dinner.

Give James His Bond

"Richy, I don't understand all these words," a frustrated Clueless complained. "You need to be a rocket scientist to understand them."

"Calm down, Clueless, it's not that complicated," Rich explained. "Here are some of the most common bond terms broken down into plain English."

1. Maturity—Often confused with puberty, this is the time when the bond will be returned with interest. Maturity dates can be under a year, and they can also be over 50 years, depending on the bond.

2. Par/Face/Principal Value—These are all names for the same thing. This is how much the buyer will receive at the maturity date.

3. Coupon Rate—This is the interest rate that will be paid on the bond. (In the olden days, bonds came with a little book of coupons, and the bondholder had to send these coupons in to receive his interest payment.)

Diversify With Mutual Funds

Mutual Friends

Clueless was having a nervous breakdown trying to decide whether to invest in stocks or bonds. Unable to make a decision, she was about to give up—until Rich explained to her what a mutual fund is. Mutual funds are a collection of stocks or bonds, all bundled into one nice little portfolio. Think of them as a bunch of mutual friends hanging out in the bar together. The catch is that you don't get to pick them. This may be a good or bad thing, depending on whether you consider yourself a financial expert or not (for Clueless, this is obviously a good thing). The stocks and bonds that go into each mutual fund are picked by a group of professional financial analysts (but remember, even their picks are educated guesses at best!), so you don't have to do anything more than determine what type of mutual fund you want to invest money in.

Your Eggs Aren't All in One Basket

Apparently, Clueless wasn't completely satisfied. She asked Rich, "Didn't you say the stock market is unpredictable, just like Stinky's foul odor? Why would these mutual funds be any better?"

Rich replied, "Mutual funds are considered a safer form of investment than individual stocks simply because we'll have a diversified portfolio. The more stocks and bonds we own in one portfolio, the less any one loss can hurt us. That's why a mutual fund is ideal for us, Clueless—because it has the diversity of many financial instruments."

Now there's something that Stinky's odor doesn't have—diversity.

Types of Mutual Funds—31 Flavors

Baskin Robbins has 31 flavors to choose from, so everyone's taste buds are satisfied. Mutual funds are quite similar to walking into a Baskin Robbins—except sometimes ice cream melts before you get to eat it. There are many types of mutual funds, but the three basic categories are:

- Money Market Funds (which usually invests in CDs and low-risk AAA-rated bonds)
- Bond Funds (which usually combine many different types of bonds)
- Stock Funds (which usually combine many different types of stocks)

Money Market Funds: Safe & Easy

This type of mutual fund—money market fund—is safe and easy. No, it's not backed by the US Government, but all financial planners will agree that money market funds are one of the safest investments around. The advantage of money market funds is that they have an interest rate that usually pays higher percentages than almost all savings accounts, which makes it ideal for a short-term savings account. The interest rates can range between 3% (on the low end) and 6% (on the high end), and can fluctuate at any given time. Some money market funds even allow you to write checks directly from your account (just like a bank!). Most funds have a minimum investment (e.g. $2,500) in order to open an account, but remember, you can pull out your money at any time. If you have a savings account with a bunch of cash in it, money market accounts are a much better alternative. To buy one, contact a mutual fund company (full contact listing in Appendix C), and speak to an advisor about the types of money market funds they have available. He or she will advise you on which ones are best for your personal situation.

Stock Funds: The Most Complex of Mutual Funds

Because everyone wants to share in a piece of the stock market, but prefers to minimize their risk, stock funds are a good way to go. But just like Baskin Robbins, where you have more flavors to choose from than you could eat in a lifetime, mutual stock funds require choices. They have the "aggressive" portfolio for the younger investor (which invests in smaller, riskier, but more profitable companies over the long-term), the "conservative" portfolio for the older investor (who usually invests in safer, lower-return stocks), and everything in between. Once you've decided you want to invest in mutual funds using stock funds, consult a financial planner or contact any of the mutual funds directly to speak with a representative who will guide you to what is most efficient and fitting for your specific situation. What defines young vs. old? Your parents don't want that question answered, and since they are probably paying for this book. . .

Liquid Money, Part II

Just like stocks, mutual funds are also liquid in nature, which means you can buy them one day and sell them the next. Unlike bonds and CDs, where your money is locked inside a vault for a selected time period, mutual funds and stocks allow you to trade your portfolio on a daily basis. And, for Rich and Clueless, this was the perfect way to be involved in the market yet have their money available in case of a real emergency—like Stinky pairing up with his best friend Stench.

Mutual Fund Fees

As ditzy as Clueless is, she knows there will be some fees associated with purchasing a mutual fund. Rich explained to her that there are three main ways mutual funds can charge you for buying. He suggested to Clueless that she avoid mutual funds with either a front-end load or a back-end load. She should stick with funds that have an expense ratio only:

Front-End Load

This is where the mutual fund will charge you an up-front fee. If Clueless is hoping to make some money to buy gas masks for everyone in the house, and invests $1,000 in a mutual fund that has a 2% Front-End Load, she will be charged $20 (2% of her $1,000 investment) at the beginning of the transaction, *before* making any money. That stinks.

Back-End Load

This is where the mutual fund will charge a back-end fee when you withdraw your money. Let's say that Clueless invests $1,000 in a mutual fund that has a 2% Back-End Load, and after a year, her investment grows to a total of $2,000. She then decides this is enough money to buy Stinky a cage for his really naughty days, so she withdraws all $2,000. She will be charged $40 (2% of her withdrawn $2,000 investment) at the end of the transaction, *after* making her money. Still stinks.

Expense Ratio

This is a certain percentage that will be charged to your account every year, based on how much your mutual fund has grown. The nice aspect of expense ratios is that you pay based on how many days you had money in the fund. Here's a "Stinky" example: Let's pretend Stinky learns how to invest, and squirts out $1,000 into a Smelly Mutual Fund, with an Expense Ratio of 4% per year. After only six months, his Smelly Mutual Fund investment grows to $2,000, and Stinky decides this is enough to buy the custom-designed skunk fan to spread his "wealth." Stinky withdraws his $2,000, and since he was only in the fund for 6 months (half a year), he is charged *half* of the annual 4% fee, which is only 2%. Stinky only pays $40 (2% of his withdrawn $2,000 investment), instead of the full annual fee of 4%, which would have been $80. Smells a lot better.

Summary

Since Clueless was developing a nervous twitch because of all the overwhelming financial information, Rich had no choice but to map out a summary of what investments were all about. Here's what he put together (see chart on next page):

Summary of Investments					
	Affordable	**Liquid**	**Risk**	**Return**	**Taxable**
Certificate of Deposit	YES	NO	LOW	LOW	YES
Bonds:					
Treasury Bills	YES	NO	LOW	MEDIUM	YES
Municipal: State, City, Local	YES	NO	LOW	MEDIUM	NO
Corporate	YES	NO	MEDIUM to HIGH	MEDIUM to HIGH	YES
Stocks	YES	YES	HIGH	VARIES	YES
Mutual Funds	YES	YES	LOW to MEDIUM	VARIES	YES

Other Investment Odds & Ends:

Be Religious

One of the best saving techniques floating around every financial planner's bag of tricks is to pay yourself first by tithing 10% of each paycheck. Most companies have an automatic direct deposit program, where you can have your paycheck transferred directly into your bank account, without your having to take a physical check to the bank. For some, this may be emotionally devastating, as they no longer will be able to frolic on their way to the bank. From a savings standpoint, this is perfect. All you have to do is open a separate savings account, and tell your company to deposit 10% into the savings account, and the rest into your checking account. When you receive your money in your checking account, it will already have had the savings deducted from it. Get used to budgeting your expenses from that account, and you won't even notice the 10% is missing! You will do yourself an enormous service by tithing to yourself first; you will be shocked to see how your savings will accumulate over time.

401(k) Retirement Plan

You're just finishing school, so why should you think about retirement now? Well, because your new employer might be giving you FREE money! With an incentive like that, why would you pass it up? A 401(k) is offered by many companies when you start working for them. This means that you have the option to put away a certain portion of your paycheck (before taxes) into an investment account (and you can choose how aggressive or conservative you want the investments to be). But here's the fun part: In most cases, your employer will match what you put away, helping you save even more! In effect, it's free money your employer is giving you, an extra way of saying "thank you" for working for their company. Here's the not-so-fun part: you can only take out your money from this 401(k) account once you've reached 59 ½. You can take it earlier, but there will be monetary penalties in most cases. Nonetheless, the 401(k) is a great opportunity to save money for down the road—with your employer's matching amount!

IRA: Individual Retirement Account

Also a retirement-driven plan, this financial instrument allows you to contribute up to $3,000 per year to your IRA. (This amount can change annually. Check with a financial planner for the current amount.) Although there are several types of IRAs, their main advantage is that all of your interest and dividends on your IRA grow tax-free, until you withdraw the money after reaching 59 ½.

Life Insurance

This is typically bought by one or both spouses when they get married. Because the world is a risky place, and any number of things can happen at any time, many people buy a life insurance policy on their spouse. That means that, if the husband or wife dies, the surviving spouse will receive a large sum of money (anywhere from $100,000 to a million dollars, depending on the type of policy you buy) to compensate for the loss of the main breadwinner's income. You buy this type of policy through a licensed life insurance agent, and then you make annual, quarterly, or monthly payments to cover your policy.

Annuity

This is often explained as reverse life insurance. An annuity pays while you live, where life insurance pays after you die. As a simple example: You can buy an annuity at the age of 40, and it will start paying you at the age of 55 on a monthly basis until you die. Even if you live until you are 200 years old, the annuity will keep sending you those monthly payments. But, if you die at 56 (man, that would be a bummer), the payments stop and can **not** be inherited or transferred to anyone else. There are many unique tax savings involved with an annuity, and it can be a great retirement instrument, but, as with all investments, consult a financial advisor on the specifics of your situation.

IV. Budgeting

If You Win the Lottery...

...you won't need to read this section. But, if you're like most people in the world, you'll need a budget. A budget means knowing how much you can financially afford—and how much you expect to spend. By having a general idea of how much you spend in the average month, you'll be able to cut costs where it matters, and save money on a disciplined plan.

Be Afraid. Be Very Afraid...

...of the two new terms you are about to learn: fixed & variable expenses. Fixed expenses are those items you can't live without, such as a place to live, a car, and for some, the overly priced drink you get at Starbucks. Variable expenses are those that only occur once in a while, and usually are not recurring charges. Examples of variable expenses are purchases of holiday gifts, As-Seen-On-TV products, and Clueless's pet skunk, Stinky. (See the investing part of this chapter if you don't remember Stinky.)

So How Do I Calculate My Expenses?

For exactly one month, keep track of all your expenses, both fixed and variable. After one month, fill in the expense amounts on the chart below, and of course, include any other fixed/variable expenses that are applicable to your circumstances:

Monthly Fixed Expenses:

Rent/Mortgage_____
Car Payment_____
Student Loans_____
Cable Bills_____
Utilities_____
Gasoline_____
Drinks & Food_____

Monthly Variable Expenses:

Movies_____
Out-of-Pocket Medical _____
Eating Out_____
Entertainment_____

Pet: Stinky_____

TOTAL EXPENSES:_____

Your Income

Now comes the fun part—payday. When you get your paycheck, calculate how much you will make each month. That means if you get paid on the 15th and 30th, add those two checks together to arrive at your total monthly income. Be sure you calculate your net pay—the amount you take home with you, after taxes have been taken out. There will be a time to seek revenge on the government, but that time is not now, so focus on calculating your net pay.

Here Comes Your Budget

As any second-grade math teacher would tell you, to calculate your budget simply subtract your total expenses from your net income. You will then be able to see if you can afford all of the expenses you put into your calculation above. If you can't, you'll have to cut corners somewhere. It's never easy to say good-bye to a pet, but Stinky might have to find a new home where he can release his repugnant odor.

The Most Important Fixed Expense: Pay Yourself

As mentioned elsewhere in this guide, most financial planners will recommend saving 10% of your take-home pay from each check. If you want to be a smart cookie—and hey, who doesn't?—take their advice and make this your most important fixed expense. Take that 10% fixed expense, pay yourself, and invest that money in savings. Stinky will find a way to live without his once-a-day sponge bath. (The real question is, will you?)

V. Health Insurance

Most students don't know much about health insurance for good reason. Students are often covered under their parents' health insurance plan until age 23. Each plan is slightly different, so check your plan accordingly, but it's for that reason that students only learn about health insurance when they get into the real world. If you think you're going to be macho and not get health insurance, just remember what happened to Estelle Hertz. Estelle decided she would not get health insurance to save a few bucks. Then came that horrible boating accident, followed by the time she forgot to turn on her gun safety feature. But when she incurred puncture wounds from her archenemy, Sharon Needles, she "paid" a visit to Dr. E. Ville, and it was a very expensive one. Don't be stingy like Ms. Hertz, because for her, it still hurts. (Get it? Estelle Hertz?) The point? Get health insurance.

What Is Health Insurance?

It is insurance against financial losses resulting from sickness or injury. Estelle liked to play with super glue. But not just any super glue. She liked Gorilla extra-strong super glue. She encountered a problem when she super glued her two left feet together. Her medical bills ran into thousands of dollars—but since she had learned her lesson from her previous experiences and obtained health insurance, the insurance company picked up most of the tab. Without having the insurance, Estelle would've been stuck in debt for years to come.

When Do You Get Health Insurance?

Anytime before you get sick. If Estelle had no insurance, and only after the superglue accident applied for a policy, the insurance companies would have turned her down faster than it took the glue to bond.

Those Darn Terms

As you might have guessed, there's a separate dictionary for the health insurance industry. Here are some of the words you might find useful:

Premium—This is the amount you pay each month to keep your insurance coverage. As logic would dictate, the better coverage you have, the higher your premium.

Deductible—The amount you pay in medical bills to be eligible for insurance to pay for the rest. If Estelle had a $500 deductible, here's what would happen. If the doctor charged her $300 for the separation of her glued feet, Estelle would have to pay all $300 herself without help from the insurance company. But if Estelle needed a full surgical procedure to separate her feet (it was a difficult procedure since she had two left feet), and it cost her $5,000, Estelle would only have to pay her deductible of $500, and the insurance company would pay the remaining balance of $4,500.

Co-Payment—The amount of money you have to pay each time you go to a doctor. This fee is usually small (e.g. $20-$40), while the remainder of the bill will be picked up by the insurance company.

Primary Care Physician (PCP)—This is your regular doctor—the one you would visit before being referred to a specialist.

In-Network Doctors—This is an exclusive list of doctors in their own network. Think of it as a fraternity or sorority that has multiple branches across the country, and when your health care plan says you can only stay "within network," that means your choice of doctors is limited to that "fraternity or sorority house."

The Full Package
If you work for a company full time, your employer will offer you the option to pay a cheaper rate for health insurance than if you were to buy it on your own. It's part of the benefit package your company wants to give you as an incentive to work for them. So how do you know which health insurance plan to choose? There are two main health plans, with a variety of others falling in between those two.

A. HMO (Health Maintenance Organization)—This is the cheapest plan with the most restrictions. When you are under an HMO, you receive a book listing all the doctors you are allowed to see. Here are the two biggest restrictions with an HMO:

1. Must Stay Within Network—It's like a covert operation for the CIA. Stay within the network, and they'll watch your back.

Step out of the network and go to another doctor—and it's like you've betrayed your country. You're on your own with nobody to financially bail you out. Be clear on this point: If you go to a doctor outside the network, the insurance company will not pay for anything.

2. Choose Only One Doctor—To further complicate matters, most HMOs require that you pick one doctor from this exclusive members-only network, and make them your Primary Care Physician (PCP). That means that when Estelle super glued her two left feet together using Gorilla-brand super glue, she would have had to go to her PCP *first*. Only then would the PCP give Estelle a referral to another doctor within the network. As you can imagine, that's a lot of legwork for a girl who just super glued her feet together.

B. PPO (Preferred Provider Organization)—At the opposite end of the spectrum, PPO's are usually more expensive than HMOs, but they offer more choices and fewer restrictions. Here's how they measure up:

1. Another Network, More Flexibility—A PPO, has a directory and network of doctors they will cover. However, if Estelle suddenly gets naughty and decides to go outside the network, the insurance company will pay for **some** of the costs. Naturally, if she stays within network, the insurance will cover **most** of her costs.

2. You're Free!—Unlike an HMO, there is no one doctor you must see first. Estelle could go straight to a specialist whose specialty is removing Gorilla-bond superglue from where it doesn't belong.

Summary Chart		
	In-Network Only	**Must Have PCP**
HMO:	YES	YES
PPO:	Flexible	NO

VI. W-2 & W-4 Forms

The Blasted IRS

Tax law is complicated, always changing, and often not applicable to your situation, coming right out of school. But there are some basics you need to know. The first important rule you must never forget: the Internal Revenue Service (IRS) is greedy.

The Government's Got It Backward

Because you're dealing with the IRS, that means things are backward. The form names are a perfect example. Anyone who passed first-grade math knows the number 2 comes before 4. But this is apparently too much for the government to handle. It would be logical for the W-2 form to come before the W-4 form, but in reality, it is reversed. The W-4 form is what you *first* fill out when you begin a job, telling the employer how much to withhold from each paycheck for the greedy government. The W-2 form (Wage and Tax Statement) is a form received *later*, summarizing all of your earnings from the past year from each employer. The W-2 form is one of the items used to calculate how much you owe in taxes at the end of the year. Just remember, it's the government, so things are done backward.

April 15: The Day of Judgment

Unless you grew up in an igloo, without access to TV, radio, or newspapers, you have probably heard of April 15—the notorious deadline for taxes due—sometimes known as "The Day of Judgment." On this day it will be decided how "good" or "bad" you've been to the government throughout the year. Every citizen pays **estimated** taxes from their paycheck (based on the W-4 form, see below). Nobody knows exactly how much is owed to the government, so employers make estimated payments throughout the year. On the Day of Judgment, the exact number is calculated and you get rewarded or punished accordingly. (Don't worry, the type of punishment referred to does not involve a weed whacker, hammer, or chain saw.)

The W-4: How Much Money to Withhold From Each Paycheck (The "Estimated" Amount)

When you start your first day on the job and the employer hands you this form to fill out, the first thing you must do is b-r-e-a-t-h-e. The form might seem overwhelming or intimidating (anything with tiny lettering sometimes causes agonizing cramps), but don't worry, here it is broken down into bite-sized chunks. Remember, the entire purpose of the form is to determine how much money to withhold for the government from each paycheck. The information below will make a lot more sense if you see the W-4 form side by side with this guide. You can easily obtain a copy from the IRS's website, www.irs.gov. There's also a copy of the 2005 form on the next few pages. These are the three main parts to the W-4:

1. Married or Single—These are two different taxable rates, so if you got hitched over summer break, you'll check the box that says you are married. Sorry, dude, the honeymoons over.

2. Withholding Allowance—Think of these as your friends. You have to enter how many "withholding allowances" you are claiming. The more withholding allowances you have, the more money for you up front. (Your employer will take less money from your paycheck to pay the greedy government.)

3. Additional Withholdings—If you're one of those people who has a hard time sleeping at night because you think you might be shortchanging the government (man, get a life), there's a line just for you. This line will allow you to have additional withholdings taken from your paycheck, allowing you to have sweet dreams, but no money to fulfill them.

The Top Half of the W-4—Recommended for Your Personal Records

The W-4 form is split in half—the top half is a worksheet that **recommends** how many allowances to claim. It gives you criteria, line by line, and walks you through the process. This total amount (on Line H) is the **recommended** amount of allowances to use on the bottom half of the W-4. This top half is for your personal use only. You will not be giving this to your employer or submitting it to the IRS. It's for your personal records, and for estimating the recommended number of personal allowances. The two lines that will most likely be applicable are:

•   Line A ("Enter 1 for yourself if no one else can claim you as a dependent")—This is basically asking you if you are living on your own and paying your own bills. If so, write a "1" on that line.

- Line B ("Enter 1 if...")—This line is one of the few that has easy-to-understand wording. For most of you just finishing school, you are single and have one job (which is the first bullet point), so you would put down a "1" as it instructs on the form.

- The rest of the lines won't be applicable unless you are married and have children. While the worksheet and forms are in the English language, you might want to consult an accountant to help you work through it.

The Bottom Half of the W-4—Mandatory to Give to Your Employer

The second portion of the W-4—the bottom half—is what you will give to your employer. Most of the lines are self-explanatory, like your name, address, and social security number. You won't need much help filling out those lines (unless you're into identity theft, in which case you'll need a lot more help than this book could ever offer). Line 5 on the bottom half (which asks for the total number of allowances claimed) is the only place it gets a little tricky. You can use the top half of the W-4 as your guide to fill out how many allowances to claim (but remember, that number of allowances is *recommended*!), or you can use the practical guide below.

General Guide for Total Number of Allowances

If you are married, working multiple jobs, or have a more complex situation, you might want to go through the top half of your W-4 with your accountant, and he can guide you in the right direction. **But, if you are single and living on your own, these general guidelines will help you decide how many allowances to write on Line 5 on the bottom half of the W-4:**

- **(The Nervous Twitch)—If you enter "0":** Your paycheck each week will be smaller, as your employer will be aggressively withholding amounts for the government from each paycheck. However, on the Day of Judgment, you will find a pretty significant refund coming your way. (Vegas, anyone?)

- **(The Boring Guy) —If you enter "1":** Your employer will be withholding the average amount, which will be very close to the actual amount you owe. As a result, on the Day of Judgment, chances are you will have a very small amount that you owe or will receive as a refund. But, either way, it won't be much. For those who don't like excitement in their lives and prefer the boring lifestyle, this approach will work best for you.

- **(The Party Animal)—If you enter "2":** You will be taking home a lot of money from each paycheck, but the government will seek revenge on the Day of Judgment. They will find you (through their spy cams and hidden microphones), making you pay the amount you truly owe. (You may want to brush up on your begging techniques, so you can get the cash from a friend.)

Employer Identification Number (EIN)
One of the very last boxes on the bottom half of the W-4 form is the EIN number. This is a nine-digit number given to organizations by the IRS. Corporations, partnerships, employers, and other business entities use these EIN numbers, and they help the IRS track what tax forms the business is required to file. The bottom line for most of you: the EIN number is not going to be applicable.

Sample W-4 Form
The image below is a blank W-4 form like you'll be given when you walk into work the first day. Notice the top half (which consists of instructions for those who triple-majored in biophysics, accounting, and space technologies and a **recommended** personal allowances worksheet). Take note of the bottom half, which says in big, bold letters: **"Employee's Withholding Allowance Certificate."** That's the part that is **required** to be filled out. Most of you will be able to use the recommended guide above for filling out this form. But, for those of you who prefer to use a high-powered microscope and dictionary on steroids to decipher instructions, feel free to read the top half.

Form W-4 (2005)

Purpose. Complete Form W-4 so that your employer can withhold the correct federal income tax from your pay. Because your tax situation may change, you may want to refigure your withholding each year.

Exemption from withholding. If you are exempt, complete only lines 1, 2, 3, 4, and 7 and sign the form to validate it. Your exemption for 2005 expires February 16, 2006. See Pub. 505, Tax Withholding and Estimated Tax.

Note. You cannot claim exemption from withholding if (a) your income exceeds $800 and includes more than $250 of unearned income (for example, interest and dividends) and (b) another person can claim you as a dependent on their tax return.

Basic instructions. If you are not exempt, complete the Personal Allowances Worksheet below. The worksheets on page 2 adjust your withholding allowances based on itemized deductions, certain credits, adjustments to income, or two-

earner/two-job situations. Complete all worksheets that apply. However, you may claim fewer (or zero) allowances.

Head of household. Generally, you may claim head of household filing status on your tax return only if you are unmarried and pay more than 50% of the costs of keeping up a home for yourself and your dependent(s) or other qualifying individuals. See line E below.

Tax credits. You can take projected tax credits into account in figuring your allowable number of withholding allowances. Credits for child or dependent care expenses and the child tax credit may be claimed using the Personal Allowances Worksheet below. See Pub. 919, How Do I Adjust My Tax Withholding? for information on converting your other credits into withholding allowances.

Nonwage income. If you have a large amount of nonwage income, such as interest or dividends, consider making estimated tax payments using Form 1040-ES, Estimated Tax for Individuals. Otherwise, you may owe additional tax.

Two earners/two jobs. If you have a working spouse or more than one job, figure the total number of allowances you are entitled to claim on all jobs using worksheets from only one Form W-4. Your withholding usually will be most accurate when all allowances are claimed on the Form W-4 for the highest paying job and zero allowances are claimed on the others.

Nonresident alien. If you are a nonresident alien, see the Instructions for Form 8233 before completing this Form W-4.

Check your withholding. After your Form W-4 takes effect, use Pub. 919 to see how the dollar amount you are having withheld compares to your projected total tax for 2005. See Pub. 919, especially if your earnings exceed $125,000 (Single) or $175,000 (Married).

Recent name change? If your name on line 1 differs from that shown on your social security card, call 1-800-772-1213 to initiate a name change and obtain a social security card showing your correct name.

Personal Allowances Worksheet (Keep for your records.)

A   Enter "1" for **yourself** if no one else can claim you as a dependent . . . .   **A** _____

B   Enter "1" if: { • You are single and have only one job; or
 • You are married, have only one job, and your spouse does not work; or
 • Your wages from a second job or your spouse's wages (or the total of both) are $1,000 or less. }   . .   **B** _____

C   Enter "1" for your **spouse**. But, you may choose to enter "-0-" if you are married and have either a working spouse or more than one job. (Entering "-0-" may help you avoid having too little tax withheld.) . . . .   **C** _____

D   Enter number of **dependents** (other than your spouse or yourself) you will claim on your tax return . . . .   **D** _____

E   Enter "1" if you will file as **head of household** on your tax return (see conditions under **Head of household** above) .   **E** _____

F   Enter "1" if you have at least $1,500 of **child or dependent care expenses** for which you plan to claim a credit . .   **F** _____
 (**Note.** Do **not** include child support payments. See Pub. 503, Child and Dependent Care Expenses, for details.)

G   **Child Tax Credit** (including additional child tax credit):
 • If your total income will be less than $54,000 ($79,000 if married), enter "2" for each eligible child.
 • If your total income will be between $54,000 and $84,000 ($79,000 and $119,000 if married), enter "1" for each eligible child plus "1" **additional** if you have four or more eligible children. . . . .   **G** _____

H   Add lines A through G and enter total here. (Note. This may be different from the number of exemptions you claim on your tax return.)   ▶ **H** _____

For accuracy,   { • If you plan to **itemize or claim adjustments to income** and want to reduce your withholding, see the **Deductions**
complete all   **and Adjustments Worksheet** on page 2.
worksheets   • If you have **more than one job** or are married and you and your spouse both work and the combined earnings from all jobs
that apply.   exceed $35,000 ($25,000 if married) see the **Two-Earner/Two-Job Worksheet** on page 2 to avoid having too little tax withheld.
 • If **neither** of the above situations applies, **stop here** and enter the number from line H on line 5 of Form W-4 below.

- - - - - - - - - - - - - - - - - -   **Cut here and give Form W-4 to your employer. Keep the top part for your records.**   - - - - - - - - - - - - - - - - -

Form **W-4**	**Employee's Withholding Allowance Certificate**	OMB No. 1545-0010
Department of the Treasury Internal Revenue Service	▶ Whether you are entitled to claim a certain number of allowances or exemption from withholding is subject to review by the IRS. Your employer may be required to send a copy of this form to the IRS.	**2005**

1 Type or print your first name and middle initial	Last name	2 Your social security number

Home address (number and street or rural route)

| | 3 ☐ Single ☐ Married ☐ Married, but withhold at higher Single rate.
Note. If married, but legally separated, or spouse is a nonresident alien, check the "Single" box. |

| City or town, state, and ZIP code | 4   If your last name differs from that shown on your social security card, check here. You must call 1-800-772-1213 for a new card. ▶ ☐ |

5   Total number of allowances you are claiming (from line **H** above **or** from the applicable worksheet on page 2)   **5** _____
6   Additional amount, if any, you want withheld from each paycheck . . . .   **6** $ _____
7   I claim exemption from withholding for 2005, and I certify that I meet **both** of the following conditions for exemption.
 • Last year I had a right to a refund of **all** federal income tax withheld because I had **no** tax liability **and**
 • This year I expect a refund of **all** federal income tax withheld because I expect to have **no** tax liability.
 If you meet both conditions, write "Exempt" here . . . . ▶ **7** _____

Under penalties of perjury, I declare that I have examined this certificate and to the best of my knowledge and belief, it is true, correct, and complete.

Employee's signature
(Form is not valid unless you sign it.) ▶   Date ▶

8 Employer's name and address (Employer: Complete lines 8 and 10 only if sending to the IRS.)	9 Office code (optional)	10 Employer identification number (EIN)

For Privacy Act and Paperwork Reduction Act Notice, see page 2.   Cat. No. 10220Q   Form **W-4** (2005)

Amounts Withheld From Each Paycheck

Congratulations! You survived the hideous first two weeks of your first job. You've filled out a gazillion forms with tiny print, learned everyone's first name (knowing their last name takes years), and have mastered the art of playing solitaire when your boss isn't looking. By the end of your second week, you have definitely earned your paycheck. (How much of it is a different story!) So, when you finally open that treasured envelope containing your paycheck, you will probably need a three-pack of smelling salts after you've fainted. Most entry-level employees are shocked to discover that from each paycheck the government and employer deduct:

- Federal Income Tax
- FICA
- Social Security Tax
- State Tax
- Court-Ordered Deductions (This is when you've done something wrong, and the courts come after your money before you even get it. An example is court-ordered payments for child support that you previously refused to pay.)

The important thing to remember is that you budget how much you can afford to pay for an apartment and other monthly expenses based on your **net income** (the amount you "take home" after taxes) instead of your **gross income** (the amount your employer said would be your salary. Of course, all the tax deductions weren't mentioned because, after all, that stuff is "obvious.")

The W-2: Summary of How Much Money You Made From Each Employer This Year

Getting your W-2 form in the mail can depress you. If you have the nightmarish job of picking up manure from farm animals, you will relive your whole year when you get your W-2. The days will flash before your eyes while the overbearing smell taunts you with each passing moment. Your W-2 is a recap and summary of all your pay stubs from throughout the year, and how much you've paid (or not paid) the greedy government. It will also outline how much money was withheld for federal tax, state tax (if applicable), social security tax, and Medicare taxes. If you thought the government was greedy before, what's your reaction now?

Sample W-2 Form

The image below is a blank W-2 Form that you will receive in the mail sometime between January and April. Most, if not all, of the boxes will already be filled in for you, giving you the financial recap of how much money you made, amounts withheld from paychecks, and various taxes withheld. Essentially, it is just information provided to you—so there's nothing to fill out.

a Control number	22222	OMB No. 1545-0008		
b Employer identification number (EIN)			1 Wages, tips, other compensation	2 Federal income tax withheld
c Employer's name, address, and ZIP code			3 Social security wages	4 Social security tax withheld
			5 Medicare wages and tips	6 Medicare tax withheld
			7 Social security tips	8 Allocated tips
d Employee's social security number			9 Advance EIC payment	10 Dependent care benefits
e Employee's first name and initial Last name			11 Nonqualified plans	12a
			13 Statutory employee Retirement plan Third-party sick pay	12b
			14 Other	12c
				12d
f Employee's address and ZIP code				
15 State Employer's state ID number	16 State wages, tips, etc.	17 State income tax	18 Local wages, tips, etc.	19 Local income tax 20 Locality name

Form **W-2** Wage and Tax Statement   **2005**   Department of the Treasury—Internal Revenue Service

Copy 1—For State, City, or Local Tax Department

So What Do I Do With It?

You have three options of what to do with your W-2 once you get it in the mail:

1. **Give It to the Accountant**—Most people have an accountant do their taxes. If you are hiring an accountant to do your taxes, simply give him the form. That's it!

2. **Do It Yourself**—There are many tax software programs on the market that walk you through doing your own taxes. Assuming you are fresh out of school and don't have many financial items to worry about, this might be the way to go. Most of the tax software programs are easy to use, especially if your situation is relatively simple. If you are brave enough for the challenge, keep the W-2 in a safe place, and when the time comes to do your taxes, the program will tell you exactly how to use the W-2 form.

3. **Throw It in the Trash**—Not recommended. If you throw it away, it just makes it even more difficult to get a copy later. And, if you're not planning on doing your taxes at all, your new address will be jail.

The Missing W-2

"Hooray, it's April 14th, and my W-2 form hasn't come in the mail! I guess I don't have to pay taxes this year!" Keep thinking like that, Bucko, and you'll be wiggling your way into an orange jumpsuit—the kind reserved for prisoners. If your employer didn't send you the W-2 form or it got lost in the mail (because you just know the mailman's secret fetish is stealing W-2s), then you are required by law to call your employer or the Internal Revenue Service (IRS) directly, at 1-800-829-1040. If it does not arrive by **February 15**, make that phone call.

Chapter 6 Homework Reading—Recommended Books

Title: *Rich Dad, Poor Dad: What the Rich Teach Their Kids about Money—That the Poor and Middle Class Do Not!*
Authors: Robert T. Kiyosaki, Sharon L. Lechter
ISBN: 0446677450
Publisher: Warner Books, Incorporated

Title: *The Wall Street Journal Guide to Understanding Money & Investing*
Authors: Kenneth M. Morris, Virginia B. Morris
ISBN: 0743266331
Publisher: Lightbulb Press, Incorporated

Title: *The Automatic Millionaire: A Powerful One-Step Plan to Live and Finish Rich*
Author: David Bach
ISBN: 0767914104
Publisher: Broadway Books

Title: *Rich on Any Income: The Easy Budgeting System That Fits in Your Checkbook*
Authors: James P. Christensen, Clint Combs, George D. Durrant
ISBN: 0875790097
Publisher: Deseret Book Company

Title: *The Money Book for the Young, Fabulous & Broke*
Author: Suze Orman
ISBN: 1573222976
Publisher: Penguin Group

Chapter 6 Summary—The Least You Need to Know in Order to Pass the Class

1) Banks generally have two types of accounts: savings and checking. Make sure your bank is FDIC insured, which means that up to $100,000 (per person) of your money is protected.

2) When writing checks be especially careful when writing out the words on the check, and keep a log of all money that goes into and comes out of your bank account.

3) When researching which credit card to get, consider factors such as the credit line, cash advances, annual fees, annual percentage rates, and introductory rates.

4) Don't take the bait of credit card companies and pay only the "minimum amount due."

5) When choosing an investment, consider the variables of how it's diversified, the risk vs. the return, its liquidity, and tax ramifications.

6) In determining a budget, calculate your variable and fixed expenses, and compare it to your income.

7) Make an informed decision about health insurance, weighing the pros and cons of HMOs compared with PPOs.

8) The W-4 Form is what you fill out on the first day of work to inform your employer of how much tax should be withheld from your paycheck.

CHAPTER 7—MONEY FOR COLLEGE:
The Scholar's Ship

"College is the best time of your life. When else are your parents going to spend several thousand dollars a year just for you to go to a strange town and get drunk every night?"

—David Wood

All Aboard!

It's no secret that college, or any form of higher education, is costly. Everyone hears about the 1600-SAT-kid who got a full scholarship to an Ivy League school. But rarely do you hear about every other type of student who gets thousands of dollars in scholarship money a year. Getting a full scholarship at the top school in the country may be difficult, but don't underestimate how deep the government's pockets really are. (They're so deep you can probably squeeze two Hummers in there with no problem.) It takes time, energy, and motivation to seek out this free money. But those who are smart—and not just the 1600-SAT people—know the money is out there. Those that have the drive to search for the money will get a nice financial ride through college—so jump on board the Scholar's Ship.

In this chapter, you will learn how to:

- Apply for grants

- Understand the purpose of the FAFSA, SAR, Pell Grant, and FSEOG

- Find and qualify for scholarships

- Determine which loans are right for your situation, including the Stafford, PLUS, Perkins, and Consolidated Loans

- Ask colleges for other ways to reduce the tuition price

Overview

Free Money? But How?
It sounds crazy at first, but it's true. Here's the birds-eye view of the available money out there:

1. Scholarships—This is a merit award for something that you can or will do. Examples include academic excellence, athletic abilities, and community involvement. But don't worry, you don't have to be the captain of the football team in order to qualify for them. (You will often hear scholarships referred to as "merit-based" awards, since they are based strictly on how well you stack up against the competition.)

2. Grants—These are given to people who qualify for them based on who they are. Such people include groups categorized by race, religion, or even small sects. You need to meet the specific criteria of the organization and apply. Many of the organizations are unknown to many, so if you take the time to find them, chances are you'll find some cash as well. (Grants are commonly known as "need-based" awards because they have a lot to do with your financial ability to pay for college. Students from low-income families often have an easier time receiving these awards.)

3. Loans—No, it's not the ideal scenario, but student loans can come at a very low interest rate and help you receive an education that will benefit you for the rest of your life. Knowing how to apply for these loans is important, and remember, you don't have to pay them for years down the road. So, if all else fails, apply for student loans with low interest rates.

4. Work-Study—It may not be free money, but it might be easy money. This type of program requires you to actually work for your money (sorry to disappoint you). The government requires colleges to have certain programs where a student can work part time, and receive, at the very least, minimum wage. To qualify, you must meet the requirements of the college, such as financial situation and good grades. It might

not sound so appealing, but jobs around the college campus can be fun and exciting. It definitely pays (pun intended!) to ask your college what types of jobs are available.

I. Grants

Overview

Here's a summary of the most important forms and terms to qualify for free grant money. One emotional success story is about a pirate named Angus who would have given his wooden right leg for some of this information.

A. **The FAFSA:** This is an acronym for Free Application for Federal Student Aid (FAFSA), and is the underlying piece of documentation you will need to complete in order to qualify for federal grants (and many state and local colleges use it as well). The information you submit on the FAFSA form will determine your Expected Family Contribution (EFC), which will be critical in determining how much award money (if any) you will receive. Think of your EFC as a measuring stick for how wealthy or poor you are. For example, a high EFC is an indicator to the government that you can afford a chauffeur and a limo, in which case you won't be getting a free ride to college. On the other hand, if you have a low EFC, this indicates to the government that you've been wearing the same smelly socks for two years straight, and need some help along the way.

B. **The SAR:** After filling out the FAFSA, a few weeks later you will automatically receive the Student Aid Report (SAR). This SAR will give you a chance to glance over the FAFSA form for any errors or modifications you want to make. You can modify or change the answers as needed, making your responses as accurate as possible. The SAR will also inform you of your Expected Family Contribution (EFC) number (aka: how smelly your socks are), and whether you are eligible for a Pell Grant.

Pell Grants: The Federal Pell Grant Program offers FREE money to undergraduate students who are in (or going to) college, based on their financial need. The U.S. Department of Education determines how much you need based on a complex set of variables. Such components include your assets, income, and how many other siblings your parents are putting through school. This information comes from the FAFSA, which determines your EFC. And your EFC is what drives the amount of money you receive from a Pell Grant. Keep in mind that a Pell Grant is not intended to pay for your entire education; it's meant to assist you in paying the huge expenses of school, which you would otherwise be unable to afford. This includes the cost of tuition and books—not air freshener for your smelly socks.

C. **The FSEOG:** For some very needy families, a Pell Grant award might not be enough to help pay for college. You will qualify for the Federal Supplemental Education Opportunity Grant (FSEOG) if you have an incredibly low EFC. These are for those people who *really* need it, and are offered to those who apply first and financially need it the most.

PART A: FAFSA

Where to Get It: Guidance Counselor's Office
Angus the Pirate thought he would have to swash-buckle his way through a frenzy of students demanding a FAFSA form. When he saw the office was empty, he lifted his eye patch in amazement. After seeing what was under the patch, the scared guidance counselor quickly offered Angus a copy of the FAFSA, but also informed him he could get it off of the Internet, at www.fafsa.ed.gov. The counselor told Angus to be sure he got the form for the right year, since little nuances and details change each year. Angus had some trouble with the fine print, considering his left eye was missing.

When to Do It
The time to complete the FAFSA form is usually between January 1 and June 30 of the year BEFORE going to college. Angus knew that he needed to complete one for each year that he hoped to get award money, but after the first year, all it would take was a simple renewal form. Noticing Angus's wooden leg, the petrified counselor told Angus that the recommended time for completing the FAFSA was in January. Angus also learned that one of the critical pieces of information he would need for the FAFSA was his parents' tax return. He knew that would be difficult for them to provide in January, since all pirates do their taxes in April. (Actually, pirates just evade taxes, but Angus was too embarrassed to tell the counselor.) The counselor suggested that Angus could *estimate* how much income they would report on the tax return, and then modify it with the exact figures (on

the SAR) at a later time. Angus felt relieved, as he could now fill out the FAFSA form in January.

What You Will Need

Angus was a clumsy pirate (he lost his eye soon after he got his hook implanted onto his stump. Get the point? Angus certainly did—right in his eye.) He didn't know what information he would need in order to fill out the FAFSA. But when he finally collected all the information, he compiled a brief list of the essential pieces of documentation needed to complete the FAFSA:

a. Your Income Tax Return
b. Your Parents' Tax Return
c. W-2 Forms - any employer you worked for is required to send you this form, which shows how much you earned
d. Bank Statements/Investment Statements
e. Federal School Code - Each prospective college you are applying to has a distinctive code, and by entering their code, you ensure that they will automatically receive a copy of the FAFSA form, allowing you to be eligible for additional money. You can include up to six prospective colleges on your FAFSA. You can get the school codes by simply calling the prospective colleges, going to their Web sites or even asking your high school counselor.
f. PIN Number (for electronic filing only!)—The Personal Identification Number (PIN) is used as your electronic "signature" when filling out the FAFSA on the Web. You can easily apply for a PIN number by going to www.pin.ed.gov or by calling 1-800-801-0576.

Filling Out the Paperwork

When Angus was going through the nitty-gritty of the paperwork, filling out the FAFSA form was overwhelming for him—especially since he had only one eye, hand, and leg. He just wasn't familiar with financial information, such as tax returns, investments, and the market value of assets. Angus saw there were about four pages of the FAFSA, ranging from very general information (e.g. social security number, marital status, and mailing address), to very technical information (e.g. your adjusted gross income, net worth, and other household information). Angus filled out as much of the form as he could, but then got frustrated because he didn't know answers to some of the questions. He took the remainder of the form to his parents. Unfortunately for Angus, his father's reply was, "College, mate? My boy won't be going to no college, yarrrr." Angus went back to his counselor and other school advisers, who assisted him in filling out the remainder of the FAFSA. Angus knew that this document is critical to getting grants, and in the long run, could save him thousands of dollars!

Before You Send It Out

Make yourself a copy of whatever you send out. You probably spent hours (if not days) working out this monster form and gathering the appropriate information. It is critical that you keep a copy of it, in case it gets lost in the mail or for verification purposes later on. Additionally, when you receive your SAR a month later, you'll want to compare the information you entered on your FAFSA to the SAR you have received. Angus made a photocopy, and hid it in the secret compartment of his eye patch. He wanted to make sure it never left his "sight" (okay, that's a corny line).

PART B: SAR

SAR — What Is It Again?

All these acronyms can drive anyone nuts, especially pirates. The Student Aid Report (SAR) is the form that you will receive anywhere between two and four weeks after filling out the FAFSA. Think of the SAR as a makeup exam, except that the preliminary answers are already filled out. Whip out the copy of your FAFSA and compare the information to the SAR (Note for Angus: don't be too hasty whipping it out; paper cuts on your eye can cause damage). Is all the information the same? Did something change in your financial situation, such as one of your parents landing a new, prestigious job as Leo the Lion in the circus? Is your income tax form finalized, and will it change your estimated amount of income for the year? These are only some of the questions you should ask yourself when reviewing the SAR. Run it by your parents or counselor, to assure you are entering the most accurate information every step of the way.

I've Been Waiting by the Mailbox, But It Hasn't Come!

If more than four to five weeks go by, and you do not receive your

SAR in the mail, try calling 1-800-433-3243, which is the Federal Student Aid Information Center. They should be able to tell you the status of the application and whether it is on its way. However, don't be like Angus, who threatened them with his hook if it didn't come within a week.

Does the SAR Have Anything Important on It?
Angus says it does (and since he's the one with the hook, he's in charge). Angus' Expected Family Contribution (EFC) was the most critical factor on the SAR. This calculation showed how much the government believed his family could afford on his college education. He was really angry when he saw his family had a high EFC (Daddy Pirate apparently was making—rather, pirating—a lot more money than Angus thought), which meant he would get very little government funding. His blood boiled and his eyes (sorry, that's eye in the singular) started to bulge. Just remember, Angus, the lower your EFC, the more money you will receive.

So How Much Money From a Pell Grant Do I Get?
If you're Angus, not much. Generally speaking, the Pell Grant amount will depend on your EFC, Cost Of Attendance (known as the "COA," which includes the cost of living and other case-specific tuition factors), and whether you are a part-time or full-time student. There's no way to know exactly how much money you will receive, but the maximum amount in recent years has been increasing, and can be a little over $4,000 per year. Remember, this is one piece of a jigsaw puzzle, and thousands of dollars each year add up to a lot of money. Once again, remember that the Pell Grant money is NOT a loan, which means it's free money, and never has to be repaid.

How Do I Collect My Money?
As the applicant, you rarely get to choose. The college you will be attending decides how to disburse your money. They might credit your tuition costs, so the grant money is automatically applied. Or, in rare circumstances, the college will send you a check for the amount, and you can use it however you choose (toward room/board, textbook costs, or tuition fees—just not new socks). You should call the financial aid office of the college you will be attending to find out what their policy is, and when they will inform you about how much money you will be receiving from a Pell Grant.

Phone Your Colleges

When you completed your FAFSA, you may have listed the colleges, and their school codes, where you were applying and hoping to get in. Once you receive the SAR, you should contact the colleges you are planning to attend, and ask for the financial aid office. Ask them if they've received your SAR, which they should have received automatically if you listed them on the initial FAFSA application. If they haven't, don't slam down the phone or threaten them with Angus' hook. Simply acknowledge that mail gets lost and ask for the address where you can send a new one. Then ask if there are any other forms you need to fill out for ADDITIONAL financial aid from that particular college. In most cases, you will need to fill out another form for each college, but don't worry, a lot of the information is repetitive, and once you've completed the FAFSA, you'll be a step ahead of the game.

PART C: FSEOG

FSEOG—Another Acronym?

This is yet another acronym, but one that helps hundreds of thousands of needy families each year. Even at the maximum, a Pell Grant won't be much help to a family in dire poverty and truly lacking the funds to pay for college. That's why the government set up the Federal Supplemental Educational Opportunity Grant (FSEOG). This is for families with extremely low EFCs, and is first given to those who are receiving Pell Grant money. This is one of those rare instances where the government is generous in giving money to people instead of taking it from them.

But What About Angus?

Angus knew there had to be some mistake on his application. After all, his parents were so poor, they had been living off of Ginger Rum for years. Angus reapplied, and was thrilled to discover that his family had a horribly low EFC. He therefore qualified for a Pell Grant and FSEOG! Way to go, Angus! Now doesn't a story like that warm your heart? It did for Angus—he even shed a tear.

How It Works

The government gives a certain amount of money to select colleges each year. Not all colleges participate, but those that do then disburse the money depending on how low a family's EFC is, and who asks for it first. Whereas for a Pell Grant, you were asking the *government* to grant you money, FSEOG is where you are asking the *college* for additional money. Angus went straight to the phone, calling the colleges he'd applied to, asking to go to the top of their list. He pleaded that he was so poor, he didn't even have enough money to buy sandpaper to "shave" his wooden leg.

What Kinda Money Are We Talking About?
Just like a Pell Grant, it varies. But in general, it can be anywhere from an extra couple hundred of dollars, all the way up to $4,000. Nothing you can retire on, but, hey, that's a heck of a lot of sandpaper!

Where to Apply For It
While the federal government gives Pell Grants, FSEOG money is given by the college itself. If the college of your choice does not participate in FSEOG, you will not be eligible to receive any of the FSEOG grant. It is therefore critical that you do your homework and ask each of your prospective colleges whether they are a qualifying college that participates in the program. Angus was pleased to discover that all his prospect colleges participated in the FSEOG program. He asked the financial aid office for an application, determined the deadline (which is usually VERY early), and then submitted the paperwork.

Standing Ovation
For a guy who lost an arm, leg, and eye, this was an eye-popping opportunity to get back on his feet (er, foot) and off to a fresh start. Come on, everyone, give Angus a hand!

II. Scholarships

Merit-Based Awards

A scholarship is a merit-based award that you can win by beating out your competition. Examples include having the best grades, athletic abilities, or the hairiest chest (guys only please) in your school. There are so many scholarships available, it can often be overwhelming. So stay focused and keep your eye on the ball, because you don't need to be a straight A student to get a scholarship award.

What You Need

There's a lot of competition out there (think lots of hairy chests). Remember, you're not the only one who is smart, good-looking, and captain of the football or cheerleading team. (Okay, maybe you are the only one, but for now, pretend you're not.) It is therefore crucial that you have all the necessary elements to make your entry package B.E.T.T.E.R. than the rest:

Biography/Resume—Some scholarships request you submit one, while others make it optional. Ask your high school counselor to assist you in writing your resume, which should include any internships (or other employment) you've held, awards you've won, and extracurricular activities. This is your time to brag. Be bold. Be proud. But if your chest really is that hairy, get a trimmer.

Essay—Uh-oh, did someone say essay? Before you faint from the thought of having to actually use your brain, remember that most scholarship essays have a limit of approximately 1,000 words. C'mon, you've written cheat sheets longer than 1,000 words! Some awards specify a topic while others do not. For essays where you develop your own topic, choose one that is of interest to you—but a word of caution: While topics such as toilet training, the death rate of bungee jumping, and the history of the tattoo may be topics you feel passionate about, the scholarship committee might feel otherwise.

Transcripts—While not often, there will be times the scholarship application asks you to send in your high school transcripts, outlining your grades and courses. Have them on file, so you can easily make copies to send out. Do yourself a favor: don't even think about altering them. You're trying to get into college, not jail.

Time—Watch those deadlines! They have a habit of sneaking up on you like elite military forces in an ambush attack. BANG! Just like that, you're eliminated.

Enclosed Cover Letter—This is a brief letter of introduction you should send with every application. Introduce yourself, explain why their scholarship is the best one on the face of the planet, why you're the ideal candidate for it, add one or two elements that make you the stud-muffin that you are, and conclude with a cordial note of appreciation for their time.

Reference Letters—These are letters of recommendation from people who know you personally. Most scholarships require a minimum of two letters, so be conservative, and get three. Whom should you ask? It's best to get a diverse group, such as a teacher, local politician, religious leader, lawyer, or other professional. Just don't get too diverse and include your uncle, whose only notable trait is that he won the gorilla chest-hair contest. In addition to including these letters of recommendation, provide a separate piece of paper with a listing of five *additional* people and their contact information (e.g. phone number, physical address, profession, and relationship to you). This shows the scholarship committee that you have a wide and diverse group of people who are ready and willing to recommend you for the award. Because, after all, you are "better" than the rest.

Where to Find Them

Believe it or not, this is the fun part. Finding scholarships is easy. The hard part is deciding which ones to apply for. There are hundreds, if not thousands, of scholarships floating around. Obviously, it's impossible to apply for all of them. Of course, you won't want to because some of them will have qualifications—many of which seem unfair—that will eliminate you (such as your great-grandmother having two unfilled cavities). Here are some of the best places to find scholarships, their requirements, deadlines, eligibility, and additional information:

1. Your local library

2. The bookstore

3. Your high school guidance counselor

4. The Internet (one of the best Web sites is www.fastweb.com)

5. Local religious institutions

A Word of Caution

One very important thing to remember: an unfortunate fact of our society is that scam artists will do anything to make a buck. That being said, there are plenty of phony scholarships out there that will insist you pay a fee to enter their "contest." They will justify their fee with a number of reasons that at times, are appealing. Before you send any money, verify their authenticity and validity.

III. Loans

What Is a Loan?

A loan is where you borrow money—either from a person or an organization—that you have to pay back at a later time. In order to make it worthwhile for the lender to temporarily lend you money, they require you to pay back the principal (the original amount), plus a designated amount of interest (a specified rate that you are charged for the use of that money). Obviously, the lower the interest rate, the better the loan. Along for the ride is an alien named Invader. He hoped for grants and a full scholarship to college, but when that didn't work out, he had no choice but to settle for loans. Once the little green man learned about all the different loans available, he got one that was out of this world.

It's Not All Bad News

Loans may not be what you *want* to do, but it might be what you *have* to do (kind of like living at home as a teenager). In an ideal world, you would receive all your tuition money from government grants and scholarships. But in the real world, those federal, state, and local programs will only pay for some of the college costs. Don't underestimate the amount of free money you can get in grants and scholarships—but don't overestimate them either. The good news is that there are several types of loans with low interest rates you can get based on your specific situation.

The Responsibility of a Loan

Invader thought he could beat the system by taking out loans and then never paying them back. He figured, "What's the worst that can happen if I don't make the payments on time?" Well, Invader, a lot of bad things can happen—and not just bad karma. Taking out a loan is a privilege, and failing to make the monthly payments after college can cause a whole series of unfortunate events. Such penalties include ruining your credit history, preventing you from ever getting a federal job, stopping you from obtaining a driver's license or other professional certification (in some states), and even having some of your salary taken away by the government. These are only some of the consequences associated with failing to pay back your loans. Invader wasn't scared by these penalties, since he planned to return to his home planet after finishing school. But once he was told the cops could come after him with weed cutters and remove his cute green antennae, he got really scared. Guess it was a language barrier.

Types of Loans

There are many types of loans, all with different details to fit different types of families (even little green ones from other planets). Outlined below are the major loans, along with the terminology you will need to know.

Loan A: The Stafford Loan

Who Gives You the Money

The Stafford loan is one of the most popular loans on the market. It can come in two forms, with the bottom line not being much different. The first is, the government lends you money directly, and when you are finished with school, you pay the government back. The second is, you borrow the money from an outside third party (e.g. banks and other organizations), and you will pay them back (instead of the government) once you complete college. Each university may choose to use the first or second method, but in the end, there isn't much difference where the loan comes from—the terms will be the same, and you will still hope to win the lottery.

Two Types of Stafford's: Subsidized vs. Unsubsidized

The first loan is subsidized, which means that interest won't start accruing until you leave college (yet another reason to cry at the commencement ceremony). Once you leave college and begin paying back the loan, you will be charged interest. On the unsubsidized Stafford loan the interest is applied (and starts accruing) from the minute you are given the money. This is not an ideal scenario, as you will be accruing interest throughout your four years in college. Invader remembered his accounting classes, and quickly calculated the interest over four years. His findings? The unsubsidized loans did not add up.

Guess Who Decides?

The unfortunate news for Invader is that the government decides which one (either subsidized or unsubsidized Stafford loan) he would receive based on his Expected Family Contribution (EFC), which was calculated from his FAFSA form (discussed above). Invader realized there was method to this madness. The students with lower EFCs usually receive the subsidized loans (so they don't have to pay more interest), while the families with higher EFCs are usually given the unsubsidized loans. (They will have to pay more interest, since the government believes they will have the means to afford it.) Since Invader's family had a high EFC (after they abduct people, they just keep the money), the government believed Invader's family could afford the hefty interest.

Who Are You Depending on?

The amount of money you receive through Stafford loans varies by individual financial cases, depending on your EFC. However, it is no secret that an independent student will receive better loans than a dependent student. Here are the technical definitions:

a. Dependent Student: This is someone who is under 24 years of age, not married, financially dependent on one (or both) parents, not a veteran of the U.S. Armed Forces, and has no dependents (e.g. they are not supporting a child or a homeless brother).

b. Independent Student: Someone with the opposite criteria of a dependent student. This someone is 24 or older, married, not financially relying on either parent, is serving or has served in the U.S. Armed Forces, and has a dependent of their own that they are financially responsible for.

Although not etched in stone, being an independent student will allow you to receive more money in loans. The government's logic is that the independent student has more responsibility weighing on their shoulders. Invader was technically a dependent student, but since he wanted more money, he insisted he was an independent student. His justification was that since he traveled through space at the speed of light, he must be "light years" older than everyone else— pushing him over the age requirement.

The $ Factor

With monetary values changing every year, the following information should be used as a starting point only. Dependent students can receive up to $2,700 for their first year in college, while independent students can receive as high as $6,700. (Now do you see why Invader wanted to be an independent student?) Notice that this is for the *first* year in college, and every year thereafter the amount you can borrow increases dramatically (for both the dependent and independent student). Check with the financial aid office of your college for the current maximum being offered.

In Your Interest

The rate of interest you pay on a Stafford loan also changes annually. It is a law that interest rates for Stafford loans are limited to 8.25%. The great news is that in recent years it has been much lower (even as low as half), making it even more affordable to borrow money. Just think, with all that extra cash, you can finally buy that matching set of glow-in-the-dark underwear and bow tie you've always wanted.

Payback

While it might be a long way down the road, thinking now about how you will repay your loans is important. Nobody wants to fork out that much money, but over time, it is manageable. Before you leave college, you will be notified about the different options you have for repaying the loan. The factors include the number of years you want to take to pay it back (ranging anywhere from 1 to 30 years) and how much money you have borrowed. Obviously, the sooner you pay it back, the less interest you will pay. While it is not necessary to know exactly what type of repayment plan you will use when leaving college, it's important to know that there are multiple options on the table. (Sorry, Invader, abducting loan collectors is not one of them.)

Loan B: The PLUS Loan

Turning the Tables

The Parent Loan for Undergraduate Students (PLUS), by its very name, suggests that this loan is not one that is taken out by the student. Rather, it's borrowed by the parents of the student, and, is also paid back by the parents. The purpose of the PLUS loan is to fill the expense gap after you've factored in money from a Pell Grant, Stafford loans, and scholarships. Like the Stafford loan, the PLUS loan is not offered for all colleges, so you'll have to call the financial aid office of your college to find out if it's available. Invader really liked the fact that his parents would be picking up a tab. He started planning his escape route, thinking of never returning home after college. Then he realized it would be quite hard for him to just blend in with the rest of society.

The Interest Factor
The highest interest rate that the PLUS loan can cost is 9%, but like the Stafford loan, it's been much lower in recent years. It varies from year to year, just like other loans, and can fluctuate depending on a variety of factors.

No Rest for the Weary
Invader learned that the downside to a PLUS loan is that as soon as his parents borrow the money, interest kicks in and, worse yet, the payments do too. His parents would then be required to pay the monthly payments (with interest) as soon as they get the money from the PLUS loan. (This is very different from the Stafford loan, which allows you to graduate college first, and only *then* begin the payments.) Invader knew that if he were to use the PLUS loan, his allowance would disappear quicker than his own abduction.

Two Types, One Set of Rules
There are two types of PLUS loans: Direct PLUS and FFEL PLUS. But the difference between these two types is so insignificant, it's almost not worth mentioning. For the most part, the terms of the loans are the same, with the only difference being who you pay back. With the Direct PLUS, it's the U.S. government you have to pay back. The FFEL PLUS loan is one where an outside third party (e.g. bank or other organization) is the one to whom you will be indebted. Don't bother losing sleep over which one to choose, since the decision is rendered for you by the college. Again, each college has their own set of rules and regulations, and will determine which type of PLUS loan you will use.

Loan C: The Perkins Loan

The Uniqueness
The Perkins loan is unique in that the college itself is the one lending you the money. When you pay back the loan, it is neither the U.S. government nor a third party you are paying; it is the college itself.

The Deadline Looms Closer

Very different from the other grants and loans mentioned earlier, the deadline for the Perkins loan is usually much earlier than the FAFSA deadline. That being the case, it's recommended that you ask the financial aid office about dates, and apply as early as you possibly can.

The Dough

Generally speaking, you can borrow up to $4,000 as an undergraduate student with a Perkins loan. As with the other loans, the amount will depend on a number of factors, but mostly, from your Expected Family Contribution (EFC), determined from your FAFSA form.

The Flexibility

The nice thing about the Perkins loan is the flexibility you have with deferment of payments (suddenly, Invader became quite interested). With other loans, it is difficult to postpone repayment of them once the time begins. With Perkins loans, there are a number of scenarios (e.g. not being able to find full-time work after college or working in select jobs for the government) where you may hold off interest accrual and actual payments for several years. You will need to notify the college of these scenarios and receive **written** permission before stopping payments.

Loan D: Consolidation Loans

One Big, Happy Family

As you've probably guessed by the name, a consolidation loan is one where all the loans mentioned above (and possibly some others as well), are rolled into one gigantic loan. The first question Invader asked is, "Why would I want to do that?" Well, here are a few reasons why a consolidated loan works to your advantage:

1. Extended Time—With each individual loan, you have a certain amount of time (e.g. 10 years) to pay the loan, but with consolidation loans, you can extend that time up to 30 years. Just think, you can be old, frail, and retired—and *still* be paying off your loans.

2. Lower Monthly Payments—The longer your plan, the lower your monthly payment will be (but you'll be paying more interest over time). This can be a huge advantage to someone who prefers lower monthly payments because they have a tight budget.

3. Only One Bill—You can eliminate getting three different bills for three different loans. With a consolidation loan, you will have only one bill each month, combining each of the other loans you borrowed. The best news is you won't have to do any of the complicated calculations to figure out how much you owe on each loan. Leave that to the government and financial aid offices so they can justify their jobs. All you have to do is find a job (or some other legal means) to pay it off.

For More Info

Check out the Loan Origination Center at 1-800-577-7392.

Poor Invader

Since poor Invader was "green" to the whole process, he had numerous questions for his counselors and parents. At times, he felt "alien" to the forms, and thought all the information he provided was an "invasion" of privacy. Finally, he was able to "abduct" his nerves, and realized that the only "unidentified flying object" was which loan to choose.

IV. It's Right Under Your Nose

Here's something that most students overlook. Many (but not all) colleges offer discounts—yes, you heard right, discounts—on their tuition price. All you have to do is ask and submit some paperwork. You're probably scratching your head over why colleges would do such a thing. Well, here are a few reasons:

1. They Want the Best—They realize that you probably have multiple acceptance letters from several colleges (being the stud that you are), so they want to give you an incentive to come to theirs.

2. You Are Special—either because you're related to the chemistry professor or because your great-grandfather attended the same college. Each college has many small programs that will qualify you as someone "special."

What to Ask for
It's okay to admit it: you're cheap. With college tuition on the rise every year, being cheap is a good quality. So, in an effort to encourage C.H.E.A.P, here is a list (although not all-inclusive) of some of the discounts you should ask colleges for:

College-sponsored grants/scholarships—Some colleges have special scholarship awards or grants that are only available to students of their college. For that reason, you may have missed them in your search for major scholarships and grants. Ask if your school has any special ones exclusively for their students.

Houses of worship—Believe it or not, if you belong to certain religious organizations, you may be able to get a discount. Not a bad time to seek out some spiritual guidance—especially if it will save you a few bucks.

Employees of the college who are related to you—Yup, that means that if Gerard the janitor is your great-uncle, you might be entitled to a special discount. Scan your family tree carefully, because one of your relatives might finally be worth something—literally.

A*lumni*—Are your parents or any siblings alumni of the college you are attending? If so, the college may want to encourage a family dynasty in their school, so they'll offer you a discount. It's now that you realize the true purpose of your parents.

P*art-time work*—If you're willing to work a certain number of hours for the college (known as the "work-study" program), you might be able to chew some of the bill off yourself. No, it's not the easy way out but, hey, it's an honest living.

The Bottom Line

Remember, this is real money you're dealing with, so don't be shy in asking everyone and anyone about ways to reduce your sizeable college bill. If you're the shy and timid kind, this is the perfect opportunity to overcome it. Call your college financial aid office, and be persistent. Ask them about every issue outlined above, and then, once they think you're about to slow down, ask them for any and all *other* information they have available about reducing your tuition. Be polite and focused, and you might be shocked to see how much money you end up saving. Remember, most people you speak to are trying to get you off the phone quickly so they can get back to their exhilarating office work. Just be persistent and assertive, without sounding like you're Freddy Kruger's most cherished disciple.

Contact Information

Federal Grants

U.S. Department of Education
www.ed.gov
1-800-872-5327

FAFSA/Federal Student Aid Information Center
www.fafsa.ed.gov
1-800-433-3243 (For a great free government publication, ask for
"The Student Guide," which lists a ton of information about student
aid, including loans, grants, and scholarships.)

Scholarships

www.collegeboard.com
www.collegenet.com
www.collegexpress.com
www.fastaid.com
www.finaid.org
www.srnexpress.com
www.scholarstuff.com

Loans & Loan Consolidation

Department of Education Direct Consolidation Loan
http://www.loanconsolidation.ed.gov
1-800-557-7392

Chapter 7 Homework Reading—Recommended Books

Title: *The Scholarship Book: The Complete Guide to Private Sector Scholarships, Fellowships, Grants, and Loans for the Undergraduate*
Authors: Daniel J. Cassidy, Ellen Schneid
ISBN: 0735203776
Publisher: Prentice Hall Press

Title: *Winning Scholarships For College: An Insider's Guide*
Author: Marianne Ragins
ISBN: 0805075216
Publisher: Henry Holt & Company, Incorporated

Title: *Scholarship Almanac 2005*
Author: Peterson's Guides
ISBN: 0768915147
Publisher: Peterson's

Title: *How to Go to College Almost for Free: The Secrets of Winning Scholarship Money*
Authors: Ben Kaplan, Benjamin R. Kaplan
ISBN: 0060937653
Publisher: HarperCollins Publishers

Title: *The Everything Paying for College Book: Grants, Loans, Scholarships, and Financial Aid -- All You Need to Fund Higher Education*
Authors: Nathan Brown, Sheryle Proper
ISBN: 1593373007
Publisher: Adams Media Corporation

Chapter 7 Summary—The Least You Need to Know in Order to Pass the Class

1) The FAFSA is the core piece of documentation you will complete in order to qualify for federal grants.

2) Your Expected Family Contribution (EFC), which is determined from the FAFSA, will directly impact the amount of Pell Grant money you will be eligible for.

3) The Federal Supplemental Educational Opportunity Grant (FSEOG) is for families with extremely low EFCs, and is first given to those who are receiving Pell Grant money.

4) While determining which scholarships to apply for, compile your biography/resume, essay, transcripts, and references.

5) Research the criteria and stipulations for Stafford, PLUS, and Perkins loans, determining which circumstance works best for your scenario.

6) Ask your college if they have specific grants and scholarships exclusive to their university, religious affiliation discounts, family-alumni markdowns, and work-study programs.

CHAPTER 8—NUTRITION & COOKING:
Body Wars

"As a child, my family's menu consisted of two choices: take it or leave it."

—Buddy Hackett

Hungry, Hungry Hippos

Most people don't know anything about nutrition or the foods they eat. Then again, most people don't care, either. For those who aspire to be groundbreaking nutritional scientists and microbiology professors (because that profession is hot these days), this chapter will do little to enhance your knowledge. However, for the rest of humanity, those who prefer to drown their steak in oil and fat and like to be served a heart-attack-waiting-to-happen in a fancy restaurant, this nutrition guide will suffice as a nice overview. It will lead into the cooking section of the chapter, compiled specifically for those who are naïve in the kitchen, recipe-handicapped, intimidated by the complicated knobs on the stove, or erroneously believe the electric knife is a chainsaw.

In this chapter, you will learn how:

- Minerals and Carbohydrates affect your body

- Fats can be good or bad

- Proteins and Fiber help build cell structure

- Vitamins are key elements of nutrition

- Cooking simple meals can be easy and fun

I. Nutrition

Most of you couldn't care less about what goes in—or out—of your body, but it might benefit the few readers who actually care about their health to explain here the very basics of nutrition. Here are the bare bones (pun intended) of nutrition. You might not be the world's leading expert in nutrition and dietary knowledge after you read this, but you sure will be a stud M.U.F.F.I.N.:

Minerals Create Molecules in the Body

Utilize Carbohydrates as Fuel and Energy

Fats: The Good, the Bad, and the Ugly

Fiber Is Food That Our Body Can't Digest

Important Proteins Help Build Cells

Nutritious Vitamins Keep Your Body Running

Minerals Create Molecules in the Body

What They Are
Minerals are elements that our bodies must have in order to create specific molecules needed for life. Minerals help the body in numerous roles, such as building strong bones and transmitting nerve impulses. In addition, minerals help make hormones and maintain a regular heartbeat. Most of the time, the food we eat provides us with these minerals. Living without a heartbeat is one thing, but no hormones? You'll never disrespect minerals again.

Two Types—Macrominerals and Trace Minerals
Macrominerals, as implied by their name, are dietary minerals needed by the human body in high quantities. Trace Minerals (also called Microminerals) are only required in very small amounts. Your body needs larger amounts of Macrominerals like calcium, sodium, and potassium. Common Trace Minerals include iron, zinc, and selenium.

Brief Explanation of the Most Common Minerals

It's quite easy to get lost in the world of minerals. Below is a list of the most common minerals your body needs. Although not all-inclusive, these are the most important and common minerals you absorb every day:

- Calcium—This is a mineral that gives strength to bones and teeth and plays an important role in muscle contraction, blood clotting, and nerve function. Remember the commercials, "Milk does a body good"? Think of the people who said it, and you'll suddenly see the correlation between calcium and beautiful bones.

- Copper—Copper acts as a catalyst in the formation of hemoglobin, the oxygen-carrying blood component. Examples of what copper does for the body include carrying oxygen in the blood stream and increasing the body's energy levels. Think of copper as the overnight delivery man—only copper doesn't have body odor.

- Fluoride—No, this is not the yucky tasting paste the dentist puts on your teeth. Fluoride is an element the body uses to strengthen bones and teeth. We get most of it from the water we drink, not from the food we eat.

- Iodine—Iodine keeps the thyroid gland healthy. The thyroid gland uses iodine to make chemicals that affect growth and help us through growth development. So, unless you want to be in the circus walking on stilts, get your daily dose of iodine.

- Iron—Although pumping iron is usually reserved for the gym, iron as a mineral is used to make tendons and ligaments. It is also critical for maintaining a healthy immune system and digesting certain foods. So pump some iron—the healthy kind.

- Magnesium—This mineral assists in the proper growth, formation, and function of bones and muscles. Magnesium is also used to convert food into energy and helps our bodies absorb calcium, potassium, and other nutrients.

- Manganese—It sustains the immune system and regulates blood sugar levels. In addition, manganese helps energy production, cell reproduction, and bone growth.

- Molybdenum—This mineral is required for the proper function of several chemicals in the human body and also helps cells grow. These chemicals help the body process iron and nitrogen in our diets.

- Phosphorus—It is a crucial component in forming healthy bones and teeth, and is also necessary for our bodies to process many foods. Additionally, phosphorus is an element of the body's energy storage system, and helps maintain healthy blood sugar levels.

- Potassium—Cells are small building blocks of the human body, and to properly function, they need to allow things to enter and leave. Cells have many ways they can control what enters and leaves, but most of those ways require potassium.

- Selenium—This mineral is a decisive part of a molecule that protects blood cells from damaging chemicals. Selenium helps our immune system produce antibodies, keeps the pancreas and heart functioning properly, and makes our tissues elastic.

- Sodium—This mineral allows us to regulate the right blood chemistry and the proper amount of water in our blood. It also allows muscles to contract normally, and is necessary to digest food.

- Zinc—This mineral is part of hundreds of different processes in the body. Its functions include helping our bodies construct and maintain DNA. In addition, this mineral helps grow and repair tissues throughout our bodies.

Utilize Carbohydrates as Fuel and Energy

The Two Groups
Carbohydrates are divided into two groups: simple and complex. Simple carbohydrates are single or double sugars. These simple carbohydrates are found in highly processed food, such as cookies, sugared cereals, sodas, and desserts. Complex carbohydrates are starches or dietary fiber, which can be found in beans, whole grains, and potatoes. Carbohydrates are needed to break down fats. During times of starvation some fats can be broken down for energy, but this is an alternate pathway for the body to produce energy.

Simple Carbohydrates
The simplest carbohydrate is glucose, which the body uses for energy. Red blood cells and much of our brain can only use glucose for energy. Glucose is a simple sugar, and other examples of simple sugars are: fructose (main sugar in fruits), sucrose, lactose (the sugar found in milk), and maltose (the sugar found in malt). Those terms don't sound so "simple."

Complex Carbohydrates (Starches)
Complex carbohydrates are often referred to as starches. A complex carbohydrate consists of chains of glucose molecules. Starches are the way plants store energy—plants produce glucose and chain the glucose molecules together to form starch. Most grains, potatoes, and plantains are high in starch. Your digestive system breaks down a complex carbohydrate into its component glucose molecules so the glucose can enter your bloodstream. Pretty "simple," eh?

Fats: The Good, the Bad, and the Ugly

Why You Need to Be "Fat"
You should eat fat for several reasons. One reason is because certain vitamins are fat soluble, which means that the only way to get these vitamins is to eat fat. Additionally, fat is a good source of energy, since it contains twice as many calories per gram as do carbohydrates or proteins. Your body can burn fat as fuel when necessary. However,

before you go on a feeding frenzy at the all-you-can-eat ice cream buffet, you might want to read the next section on Bad Fats.

Bad fats: Saturated & Trans Fats

Saturated Fats
Saturated fats are solid at room temperature and turn to oil when heated. Most saturated fats are animal in origin, from meat, poultry, and dairy products. Saturated fats are known as "bad fats" and should be restricted as much as possible. Saturated fats raise cholesterol and triglyceride levels in the blood, and some research shows that they interfere with the body's immune function. Two vegetable sources you want to avoid are coconut oil and palm kernel oil, which are high in saturated fat even though they're plant oils. Saturated fats are mainly found in animal products, such as meat, dairy, eggs, and seafood. So be careful with products high in saturated fats—they are the jerks in the "fat" class who give the other fatties a bad name.

Trans Fats
Trans fats were invented when scientists began to "hydrogenate" liquid oils so they could withstand the food production process better and maintain a better shelf life. Through hydrogenation, trans fatty acids are created. Trans fatty acids are found in many packaged foods, such as cookies, crackers, fried foods (e.g. French fries), and microwave popcorn. This is a second fat that ought to be grounded for misbehavior.

Good fats: Monounsaturated & Polyunsaturated Fats

Monounsaturated Fats
This good fat lowers LDL cholesterol (the bad cholesterol) and increases HDL cholesterol (the good cholesterol). Nut, canola, and olive oils are high in monounsaturated fats. These are the "healthiest" choices of oils, since they decrease LDL levels or "bad" cholesterol.

Polyunsaturated Fats
These fats originate from plant sources and are liquid at room temperature. They are considered to be a "healthier fat" because they help lower total cholesterol. Vegetable oils, such as safflower, sunflower, sesame, cottonseed, and corn, are polyunsaturated fats.

Ugly fats: Ever hear the expression, "It's not over until the fat lady sings?" Well, that's an ugly fat.

Fiber Is Food That Our Body Can't Digest

What Is a Fiber?
It's a broad name given to any food component we eat that our bodies cannot digest. The three fibers we consume on a regular basis are pectin, hemicellulose, and cellulose. When we eat fiber, it simply passes straight through, untouched by the digestive system. You're dying to know more about these groups of fibers, so here they are, broken down into basic definitions.

Hemicellulose and Pectin
Hemicellulose is found in different grains, like wheat. Pectin is found most often in fruits, and is soluble in water but non-digestible. Pectin is normally called "water-soluble fiber" and forms a gel.

Cellulose
This fiber is the structural component of plants, which gives a vegetable its shape. Cellulose is a complex carbohydrate (but nothing about nutrition so far has been too "complex"), and is a chain of glucose molecules. Some animals and insects can digest cellulose. Both cows and termites have no problem with it because they have bacteria in their digestive systems, which secrets enzymes that break down cellulose into glucose. Human beings have neither the enzymes nor the beneficial bacteria, so cellulose is fiber for us.

Important Proteins Help Build Cells

Proteins & Amino Acids
Protein is any chain of amino acids. An amino acid is a small molecule that acts as the building block of any cell. Carbohydrates provide cells with energy (see above), while amino acids provide cells with the building material they need to grow and maintain their structure. Amino acids all contain an amino group (NH2) and a

carboxyl group (COOH), which is acidic. In case you're curious, the human body is constructed of 20 different amino acids.

Amino Acids: The Nonessential Ones

We know that the term "nonessential" might lead you to believe they're not important and that you can skip this section. Sorry to burst your nutrition-fantasy bubble, but the real meaning of nonessential amino acids is that your body can create them out of other chemicals found in your body. They're called "nonessential" because you can make them yourself. Here is a brief list of some of the most common nonessential acids:

- Alanine
- Asparagine
- Aspartic Acid
- Cysteine
- Glutamic Acid
- Glycine
- Proline
- Serine
- Tyrosine

Amino Acids: The Essential Ones

Essential amino acids cannot be created from chemicals in your body, and the only way to get them is through protein in your food. Here is a brief list of some of the essential amino acids:

- Isoleucine
- Leucine
- Lysine
- Methionine
- Threonine
- Tryptophan
- Valine

Sources of Protein

Protein can come from both animal and vegetable sources. Most animal sources, like meat, milk, and eggs, provide complete protein, since they include all of the essential amino acids. Vegetable sources usually are low in or missing certain essential amino acids. However, different vegetable sources are deficient in different amino acids, and by eating a variety of foods you can get all of the essential amino acids throughout the course of the day. The digestive system breaks all proteins down into amino acids that can enter the bloodstream. Cells then use the amino acids as building blocks.

Nutritious Vitamins Keep Your Body Running

What Are Vitamins
Vitamins are small molecules that your body needs to keep itself running properly. Vitamins are a diverse class of at least 13 known organic compounds that are involved in almost every metabolic process in the human body. Vitamins do not provide energy directly, but they help control energy-producing processes.

Knowing Your ABCs
Listed below is a brief overview on each of the major vitamins. However, it's important to understand that this overview guide is just that: an overview. Consult your physician to determine which vitamins (and their dosages) are right for you.

Vitamin A: This one improves vision, supports the immune system, and aids in the growth and maintenance of bones, cells, and skin.

Vitamin B1 (also called thiamin): This keeps your appetite consistent. Otherwise, you'd be eating a slice of pizza one day and a 33-ounce steak the next. (If you ever ate a 33-ounce steak, you were probably fasting the week prior to eating it.)

Vitamin B2 (also called riboflavin): This one supports energy metabolism, assists your eyes, and works for healthier skin.

Vitamin B3 (also called niacin): This vitamin is made by your body, and maintains metabolism, improves the condition of skin, and supports the digestive and nervous systems.

Vitamin B6: This allows you to think more clearly and supports the immune system and hormone activity.

Vitamin B12: This vitamin protects your nervous system and supports both bone growth and metabolism.

Folate (also called folic acid): This vitamin is essential for new cell development.

Vitamin C: Vitamin C helps prevent disease and infection and promotes the body's absorption of iron. It also helps bones grow, forms scar tissue, and strengthens blood vessels.

Vitamin D: This one fortifies the bones and plays supporting roles in the maintenance of your brain, pancreas, skin, muscles, reproductive organs, and immune system.

Vitamin E: Vitamin E gives you healthy skin, heals scars, and even protects the lungs from air pollutants.

II. Recipes: Duck, Duck, Goose

Love at First Bite

Face it. Some people like to watch the Food Channel while others prefer to eat it. If you're really interested and intrigued by cooking, you'll open a cookbook or watch the Food Channel for more dazzling and impressive recipes. The following recipes are easy, short, quick, and tasty. The criteria was that every recipe be limited to under ten ingredients, less than five steps, and total preparation time of under 40 minutes. Since cooking might scare some of you, each recipe is introduced with a sprinkle of humor. Here are ten recipes that are so easy to follow, anyone can make them.

Recipe #1: Chicken Run

Two foreigners arrive in the United States for the first time, and are walking through New York City.

One says to the other, "I understand that the people of this country actually eat dogs."

"Odd," her companion replies, "but if we shall live in America, we might as well do as the Americans do."

Nodding, the first lady points to a hot dog vendor and they both walk toward the cart. "Two dogs, please," she says.

The vendor wraps both hot dogs in foil and hands them over. Excited, the foreigners hurry to a bench and begin to unwrap their food. The first lady opens hers. She blushes and then, staring at it for a moment, leans over to her friend and whispers cautiously, "What part did you get?"

How Many People It Serves: 5-7
Method of Cooking: Microwave
How Long It Takes: Under 30 Minutes
What You'll Need:

1. Two and one-half pounds (2 ½) of chicken parts, skinned
2. One-half (1/2) cup of chopped onion
3. One (1) cup of sliced mushrooms
4. Fifteen (15) ounces of spaghetti sauce (approximately one jar).

What to Do:

Step #1: Place chicken in a microwave-safe 12 x 8 dish. (For fastest results, arrange the thicker pieces of chicken toward edges of the dish.) Sprinkle the mushrooms and onions evenly on top of the chicken, then pour the spaghetti sauce over it.

Step #2: Cover with Saran Wrap or waxed paper. Microwave for approximately twenty (20) minutes. For best results, rearrange the chicken 2-3 times during the cooking process.

Step #3: After microwaving, let it sit covered on the counter for approximately 5-10 minutes, or as needed, until chicken is fully cooked and no longer pink in center.

Recipe #2: Meat & Potatoes

Two friends were standing in line at a fast-food restaurant, waiting to place their orders. A big sign was posted. "No bills larger than $20 will be accepted."

The woman in front of them, pointing to the sign, remarked, "Believe me, if I had a bill larger than $20, I wouldn't be eating here."

How Many People It Serves: 4
Method of Cooking: Microwave
How Long It Takes: Approximately 30 minutes
What You'll Need:

1. Three (3) pounds of beef pot roast
2. Four (4) potatoes (slice into 2-inch portions)
3. Five (5) carrots (slice into thirds)
4. (Optional for more flavor) One & one-fourth (1¼) ounces of onion soup mix

What to Do:

Step #1: Put the pot roast into a microwave-safe 12 x 8 dish and surround the roast with the carrots and potatoes, spreading them out evenly.

Step #2: Sprinkle the onion soup mix over the roast, carrots, and potatoes. Cover the dish.

Step #3: Microwave for approximately thirty (30) minutes.

Recipe #3: Rib, I

One day, John and Chris went to a restaurant for dinner. As soon as the waiter took out two steaks, John quickly picked out the bigger steak for himself.

Chris wasn't happy about that, "When are you going to learn to be polite?"

John replied, "If you had the chance to pick first, which one would you pick?"

Chris said, "The smaller piece, of course."

John replied back, "What are you whining about then? The smaller piece is what you want, right?"

How Many People It Serves: 4
Method of Cooking: Microwave
How Long It Takes: Under 40 minutes
What You'll Need:

1. Two (2) pounds of beef short ribs
2. Four (4) ears of corn (cut ears in half to make two small ears each)
3. One and one-half (1 ½) cup of BBQ sauce

What to Do:

Step #1: Put the ribs around the edges of a microwave-safe 12 x 8 dish and place the half ears or corn in the center.

Step #2: Pour the BBQ sauce over the ribs, using a knife to spread it evenly. Cover the dish with Saran Wrap.

Step #3: Microwave for approximately forty (40) minutes.

Recipe #4: Corn Soup

"The most remarkable thing about my mother is that for 30 years she served the family nothing but leftovers. The original meal has never been found."—Sam Levinson

How Many People It Serves: 4-5
Method of Cooking: Stovetop
How Long It Takes: 30 minutes
What You'll Need:

1. Six (6) cups of corn (frozen or canned, drain if canned)
2. Five (5) cups of water
3. Two (2) teaspoons of soy sauce
4. One-half (½) teaspoon of sesame oil
5. Two (2) tablespoons of sherry wine
6. One-half (½) cup chopped onion

What to do:

Step #1: Place all ingredients in a pot, place pot on stovetop burner, and turn the burner on high.

Step #2: When the soup begins to boil, turn to low and simmer for ten minutes.

Step #3: Puree the soup in a blender until creamy and serve.

Recipe #5: Festive Salad

A family of tomatoes was walking down the street when the baby tomato started to lag behind. The big father tomato walks back to the baby tomato, stomps on her, squashing her into a red paste, and says, "Ketchup!"

How Many People It Serves: 8
How Long It Takes: 10 minutes
What You'll Need:

1. Three (3) bags of lettuce (rinsed and drained)

2. One (1) mango (cut into bite sized pieces)
3. Two (2) cups of craisins (dried cranberries)
4. Two (2) cups of fresh strawberries (sliced)
5. One-half (½) cup chopped onions
6. One (1) cup of slivered almonds

Dressing:

1. One-half (½) cup of sugar
2. One (1) teaspoon of salt
3. Three-fourths (¾) cup of oil
4. One-third (1/3) cup of balsamic vinegar

What to Do:

Step #1: Mix all the dressing ingredients together in a bowl.

Step #2: Put the first six ingredients into a large bowl.

Step #3: Pour the salad dressing over the ingredients in the large bowl and mix gently. Serve immediately.

Recipe #6: French Toast

When the waitress brought him the soup he'd ordered, the man was a bit dismayed. "Good heavens," he said, "what is this?"
"Why, it's bean soup," she replied.
"I don't care what it's been," he sputtered. "What is it now?"

How Many People It Serves: 2
Method of Cooking: Stovetop
How Long It Takes: 30 minutes
What You'll Need:

1. Three (3) eggs
2. Four (4) slices of bread
3. Two (2) tablespoons of sugar
4. Light dash of vanilla

What to Do:

Step #1: In a small bowl, mix all ingredients together except for the bread.

Step #2: Soak the bread in the mixture (up to ten minutes).

Step #3: Spray skillet with cooking spray and place bread in skillet.

Step #4: Place skillet on stovetop burner. Turn burner on medium-high heat and cook each side of bread until golden brown. Serve with butter and syrup.

Recipe #7: Fish in the Sea

"A bad day of fishing is better than a good day of work."—Author Unknown

How Many People It Serves: 4-6
Method of Cooking: Oven
How Long It Takes: 30 minutes
What You'll Need:

1. Two (2) to three (3) lbs. of Salmon fillet
2. Ranch salad dressing (enough to cover fillets)
3. One (1) cup shelled pistachio nuts

What to Do:

Step #1: Preheat oven to 350°.

Step #2: Wash and dry salmon fillet. Coat top and bottom with ranch dressing and place fillet in ovenproof pan or dish.

Step #3: Crush nuts and sprinkle over fish. Bake in oven for 30 minutes or until you can flake the fish with a fork.

Recipe #8: Macaroni Salad

"Daddy, are caterpillars good to eat?" asked Timmy.

Daddy replied, "Have I not told you never to mention such things during meals!"

Mommy chimed in, "Why did you ask that, Timmy?"

Little Timmy answered, "It's because I saw one on daddy's lettuce, but now it's gone."

How Many People It Serves: 6
How Long It Takes: 15 minutes
What You'll Need:

1. One (1) 12-oz. box of elbow macaroni
2. One (1) teaspoon of celery salt
3. Two (2) teaspoons of garlic powder
4. One-half (½) teaspoon of onion powder
5. Two (2) teaspoons of mustard
6. Three (3) tablespoons of mayonnaise
7. Dash of pepper
8. One (1) small cucumber (chopped)
9. One (1) small red pepper (chopped)

What To Do:

Step #1: Boil macaroni according to instructions on box. Drain in colander.

Step #2: Mix chopped red pepper and cucumber into macaroni with the rest of the ingredients. Refrigerate.

Recipe #9: Corned Beef Sandwich

The next time someone says to you, "I thought you were trying to get into shape," you can respond with, "I am. The shape I've selected is a triangle."

How Many People It Serves: 3-4
Method of Cooking: Oven
How Long It Takes: 15 minutes
What You'll Need:

1. Eight (8) teaspoons of spicy mustard
2. Ten (10) ounces of freshly sliced corned beef
3. Six (6) slices of bread
4. One-half (1/2) pint of coleslaw

What to Do:

Step #1: Preheat oven to 350 degrees.

Step #2: Create the sandwich by spreading the mustard on each slice of bread. Divide the corned beef among three slices of bread. Add two spoonfuls of coleslaw to the three slices.

Step #3: Place sandwiches into the oven on a baking sheet. Bake until the bread is lightly toasted.

Recipe #10: Apple of My Pie

Bob visits his grandmother in the nursing home. It turns out that she is taking a nap, so he just sits down in a chair in her room, flips through a few magazines, and munches on some peanuts sitting in a bowl on the table. Eventually, Bob's grandmother wakes up, and Bob realizes he's accidentally finished the entire bowl.

"I'm so sorry, grandma, I've eaten all of your peanuts!"

"That's okay, Bobbie," she replies. "After I've sucked the chocolate off, I don't care for them anyway."

How Many People It Serves: 3-5
Method of Cooking: Microwave and Oven
How Long It Takes: 20 Minutes
What You'll Need:

1. One-half (1/2) teaspoon of cinnamon
2. Ten (10) slices of bread
3. Two (2) tablespoons of butter
4. One (1) package of frozen apples
5. Five (5) slices of cheese

What to Do:

Step #1: Combine the frozen apples and cinnamon in a microwave-safe bowl. Place them into the microwave on defrost for 8-10 minutes.

Step #2: Place the cheese onto five slices of the bread, and spread the apple mixture evenly onto the cheese. Place the other pieces of bread on top, creating sandwiches.

Step #3: Spread the butter on the outer sides of the bread, and broil in the oven until the cheese is melted and the bread is lightly toasted.

Chapter 8 Homework Reading–Recommended Books

Title: *Rachael Ray's 30-Minute Get Real Meals: Eat Healthy without Going to Extremes*
Author: Rachael Ray
ISBN: 1400082536
Publisher: Crown Publishing Group

Title: *The Mix-it-up Cookbook: Make More than 100 Dishes from 18 Basic Recipes*
Authors: Staff of American Girl, Tracy McGuinness
ISBN: 1584857420
Publisher: Pleasant Company Publications

Title: *The Ultimate 30-Minute Cookbook: Over 220 Delicious Dishes You Can Cook in Less Than Half an Hour*
Authors: Jenni Fleetwood, Linda Fraser
ISBN: 0760748543
Publisher: Barnes & Noble Books

Title: *Complete Idiot's Guide to Total Nutrition*
Authors: Joy Bauer, M. S. Bauer
ISBN: 0028644247
Publisher: Alpha

Title: *Eat to Live: The Revolutionary Formula for Fast and Sustained Weight Loss*
Author: Joel Fuhrman, Mehmet Oz
ISBN: 0316829455
Publisher: Little, Brown & Company

Chapter 8 Summary—The Least You Need to Know in Order to Pass the Class

1) Minerals are elements that our bodies must have in order to create specific molecules needed in the body.

2) Carbohydrates are divided into two groups: simple and complex, and our body uses them for fuel and energy.

3) Bad fats are Saturated and Trans Fats, while the good fats are Monounsaturated and Polyunsaturated.

4) Fiber is a broad name given to the things we eat that our bodies cannot digest. The three main fibers we eat on a regular basis are Pectin, Hemicellulose, and Cellulose.

5) Protein is a chain of amino acids, which are small molecules that act as the building blocks of a cell.

6) Vitamins are small molecules that your body needs to keep itself running properly.

7) If you're looking for recipes that are limited to under ten ingredients, fewer than five steps, and total preparation time of under 40 minutes, use the top ten recipes listed in the pages above.

CHAPTER 9—IDENTITY THEFT:
My Secret Identity

"You were born an original. Don't die a copy."

—John Mason

Carbon Copy

You see it in the movies, nightly news, and—gulp—even Oprah. Identity theft is becoming more prevalent, especially with the new age of Internet scams. It's one of those things you hope you will never have to deal with, but an issue you should know plenty about—in the unfortunate event that it does happen. You don't have to buy surveillance cameras, night-vision binoculars, or a shotgun (although that could help in shutting up your neighbor's annoying goat), but do be aware of your surroundings. You don't have to get neurotic about identity theft—just knowledgeable enough so that there's not two of you walking around out there.

In this chapter, you will learn how:

- Thieves obtain your personal information

- Crooks will use it to ruin your credit

- Certain signs point to your being a victim

- You should react to discovering you've been a victim

- To live a preventative lifestyle

I. How It Happens

Background
Imagine a new you, someone who has taken on your identity, using your name, social security number, credit cards, and other personal information. Armed with critical information about you, thieves can open new accounts and write checks in your name, all while destroying your credit history and personal life. Take a step back for a moment and realize this is not the newest blockbuster in Hollywood. This is real—and quite scary. Learn from the case of Ms. Sing, a woman who came home after a hard day of work, only to find her mail stolen—along with her identity.

Can It Be Prevented?
Identity theft is like chickenpox—you can't really control whether you get it or not, but you can significantly reduce the risk if you take the necessary precautions. And if you've never had chickenpox before—it itches. Ms. Sing didn't know the basics of identity theft, and had she "armed" herself with this knowledge, she would have had a "leg up" on the situation. The best part is that you don't have to pay an arm and a leg to prevent identity theft.

What the Bad Guys Need
All they need is one piece of important information, like a social security number. Once they have it, they can easily obtain your address and other information, then open bank accounts and credit cards under your name. But it's not just a social security number they're after. They will look for any piece of sensitive information (e.g. your credit card or bank account number). Ms. Sing's poor personal hygiene was sensitive information, but it's not the kind the crook used to smell her out.

How They Get It
Identity thieves are getting more clever as time passes. They can obtain this sensitive information by stealing employee files, your wallet, or sensitive mail that is sent to your home (such as credit card offers). They might complete a "change of address" form for you, rerouting your mail to another location. And the real hard-core thieves go through the trash, looking for old receipts, bills, and mail that might contain this information (and you thought Oscar the

Grouch stayed on Sesame Street). In the case of Ms. Sing, the crook stole some sensitive letters from her mailbox. Able to open Ms. Sing's letters, the crook obtained Ms. Sing's social security number—a ticket to a new identity.

What Can They Do With It?

You know all those things you'd love to do, but just don't have the money to do them? Like a new car, a lavish vacation, and spiffy new clothes—that's what they're doing with your identity. They take on your identity, accruing debt that will ultimately be your responsibility. Poor Ms. Sing was a victim at the highest level. The thief charged as much as she could to a credit card in Ms. Sing's name, including a home surveillance system, a vicious German shepherd watchdog, and a new LoJack system for her new car. (She was paranoid that someone would steal it.) She also took out loans in Ms. Sing's name and changed the address of her credit card bill, so that Ms. Sing wouldn't notice she had been defrauded until it was too late. But the worst was yet to come. The thief was arrested for mugging an old lady on the street, and after she was arrested, she gave Ms. Sing's name to the police. The next day, the crook was released on bail, and when the crook failed to show up for her court date, a warrant was issued for Ms. Sing's arrest. Talk about jailbait.

Symptoms of the Crime

There are a few things that can tip you off that something fishy is happening. Review your credit card bills each month, looking for strange charges or purchases that you don't recall making. Be aware of when you should receive your credit card bill in the mail, and if it seems to be late, don't think you're getting lucky and they forgot about you. Call your credit card company and ask when you can expect to receive it. On the flip side, if you suddenly get a new credit card that you did not apply for, be suspicious and inquire about it. Ms. Sing would have loved to have done all that—but she was too busy being hauled off to jail for a crime she didn't commit.

The Credit Report

The importance of credit reports was discussed in other chapters, but here is where it really comes into play. Contact any of the three credit agencies: Equifax (1-800-525-6285); Experian (1-888-397-3742); or Transunion (1-800-680-7289), requesting your credit report. This report will reveal most illegal activity, if any, that is happening on your account. Look for bank accounts that are not yours, credit cards you've never heard of, loans you didn't apply for, phony addresses in exotic Weed, New Mexico, and any other information that looks strange. Due diligence in examining these reports will give you a great advantage in catching these thieves, if indeed you are a victim. When Ms. Sing was given one phone call in the jailhouse, she didn't call her Aunt Bertha—she called the first credit agency that came to mind, knowing she'd be able to instantly spot the fraudulent activity.

II. Actions to Take When a Victim

There's nothing worse than falling prey to identity theft, and then not knowing what to do about it. So, if you find yourself an unfortunate victim, don't let that thief get away easily. Ms. Sing may have been duped, but she wasn't stupid. She learned all about her rights and exactly what she needed to do in order to S.T.E.A.L. her identity back.

Signal a Fraud Alert on Your Credit Reports

Tell the FTC (Federal Trade Commission)

Extinguish Any Fraudulent Accounts

Alert the Local Police Department

Live a Precautionary Lifestyle

Step #1: Signal a Fraud Alert on Your Credit Reports

Contact the Agencies

The first thing Ms. Sing did was contact one of the three major credit reporting agencies (listed in the section above), and let them know that her identity had been stolen, and that she wanted to place a fraud alert on her credit report. This alert prevented the thief from starting new accounts in her name. That's why she made it her only phone call from jail—even if Aunt Bertha would later scold her.

The Credit Reports

Once you notify one of the agencies, it will automatically alert the other two agencies, and you will be sent free copies of your credit report. Once you receive them, you should review the reports for inaccurate information, such as your social security number, address, and any accounts that are unfamiliar to you. For example, if you see a new account opened with an address in Las Vegas, it's probably a good indication that someone is partying without you. Ms. Sing ordered credit reports periodically during her first "recovery" year, just to be sure that identity theft was not recurring. She wanted to know that if, in fact, someone had won the jackpot in Vegas in her name, she would get a piece of it!

Step #2: Tell the FTC (Federal Trade Commission)

The Federal Trade Commission works for the consumer, to protect people and prevent identity fraud. You should inform the FTC (see the contact information at the end of this chapter), as it will help them find the perpetrators who did this to you. There's no charge for this service and they're there to help, so you might as well let them.

Step #3: Extinguish Any Fraudulent Accounts

Credit Cards & Banks

Once Ms. Sing discovered what the thief had done to her, it was time to erase the mess. Using her credit reports from the credit agencies, she was able to determine which credit cards, bank accounts, and other services were affected. Those that were fraudulently opened or had deceitful activities occurring in them were instantly closed. She contacted her credit card company and bank, also informing them of the situation.

Phony Checks

You can easily find out if your checks are being fraudulently used by calling SCAN (Shared Check Authorization Network) at 1-800-262-7771. If your checks have been stolen, and someone is writing fraudulent checks from your account, you should notify several check verification companies, such as Telecheck, Certegy Inc., and International Check Services. (See the end of this chapter for full contact information.) Tell them your checks have been stolen and are being used, and that they should prevent their retailers from accepting those checks. Ms. Sing was lucky in that the thief preferred plastic over paper, choosing only to use credit cards, not checks.

Step #4: Alert the Local Police Department

Contact your local police department, file a report, and record all the information and details. You should request a copy of the police report (or get the report number), as it can come in handy in the future. Creditors may request that you pay your "phony" bills, and showing them the police report will prove that you took credible action in attempting to rectify your credit. Ms. Sing refused to pay for the German shepherd watchdog that the thief bought in her name, and when the company threatened to "release the hound" should they not receive payment, she showed them a copy of the police report (along with the stunning video of when she was shackled with a big ball and chain). To express their apologetic feelings, the company shipped a German shepherd to Ms. Sing, free of charge. The only problem? It was trained to attack strangers—and it wasn't familiar with Ms. Sing.

Step #5: Live a Precautionary Lifestyle

It's a shame you have to live your life in this manner, but sometimes, keeping your personal information private (like that ingrown toe nail Ms. Sing never told anyone about) is the best way to protect yourself. Here are some tips in how to keep your personal information to yourself.

Impersonators Over the Phone

Identity thieves love to call you, pretending they are representatives of your bank or credit card company, with a story saying they need to verify your information because their system broke down. You should be very wary of anyone who calls you asking for personal information. You should get their identification number, saying you will call them back. Hang up, call the phone number of your institution (using the number from the phone book), and verify that they really are who they say they are. You can then ask to be transferred to the person who initially called you, apologizing for the inconvenience. Ms. Sing did this all the time—until the German shepherd bit off eight of her ten fingers when she let it lick peanut butter from her hands. Down to two fingers, Ms. Sing decided it would be best if she didn't speak to anyone over the phone—especially those sympathetically offering more free pets.

Revealing Information on Forms

When writing any personal information on an application, you should always ask why that information is necessary and how it will be kept safe and confidential. Concern about revealing personal information is especially critical when it comes to social security numbers. Anytime you are asked to give your social security number, you should immediately question the reason. Additionally, ask what would happen if you don't give your social security number. Only when it is absolutely vital for your application and you are comfortable with the answer about how it will be safeguarded, should you give the information.

When You Go on Vacation...

...don't let your mail sit in the mailbox. This is an open invitation for a sleaze bag to go into your mailbox and steal important information that could contain your social security number and other personal information. To prevent this, contact the US Postal Service at 1-800-275-8777, and ask them to hold your mail until your vacation is over. Alternatively, you could ask a friend or trusted neighbor to pick it up at night. This way, your mailbox won't be overstuffed, and you will not receive any unwanted attention.

Buy a Shredder

Certain documents that you throw out may have sensitive information. It's been recommended by experts to shred these papers before placing them in the trash. You never know who might be going through your garbage.

The Danger of the Internet

The Internet poses the greatest threat for identity theft. Information is easily hacked, and this can cause many problems. Although there is no absolutely foolproof method of preventing identity theft from the Internet, you can take precautionary steps to protect yourself. You should regularly update your virus protection software, assuring it is the most up-to-date version.

E-Mail Attachments & Links

Don't open attachments or click on links in e-mails from people you don't know. Often you may get an e-mail with a link to a seemingly legitimate Web site (like a bank or company with whom you have an authentic account). These links will take you to Web sites that look and feel like real Web sites—but beware!—they are phony. The easiest way to identify the real from the fakes is to look at the Web address in the menu bar. Does is say the real name of the company or does it have a lot of mumbo jumbo? Ms. Sing would have been happy to give you a live demonstration, but she didn't heed advice, and once again, fell prey to identity theft. When last heard from, she was on the Internet, buying a guillotine to behead the thief who stole her identity. She gave her credit card information through an unsecured server and—POOF!—just like that, she went missing.

Contact Information for Identity Theft

Federal Trade Commission—Identity Theft Clearinghouse Division
600 Pennsylvania Avenue, NW
Washington, DC 20580
1-877-IDTHEFT (438-4338)

SCAN
1-800-262-7771

TeleCheck
1-800-710-9898 or 927-0188

Certegy, Inc.
1-800-437-5120

International Check Services
1-800-631-9656

Chapter 9 Homework Reading—Recommended Books

Title: *50 Ways to Protect Your Identity and Your Credit: Everything You Need to Know About Identy Theft, Credit Cards, Credit Repair, and Credit Reports*
Author: Steve Weisman
ISBN: 013146759X
Publisher: Pearson Education

Title: *Preventing Identity Theft for Dummies*
Author: Michael Arata
ISBN: 0764573365
Publisher: Wiley, John & Sons, Incorporated

Title: *The Real U Guide to Identity Theft*
Author: Frank Abagnale
ISBN: 1932999019
Publisher: Real U Guides

Title: *Identity Theft Protection Guide: Safeguard Your Family, Protect Your Privacy, Recover a Stolen Identity*
Author: Amanda Welsh
ISBN: 0312327099
Publisher: St. Martin's Press

Title: *Credit Repair Kit*
Author: John Ventura
ISBN: 0793180600
Publisher: Dearborn Trade

Chapter 9 Summary—The Least You Need to Know in Order to Pass the Class

1) Identity thieves look for sensitive information about you, such as your credit card information, bank account numbers, or social security number.

2) Thieves obtain information by stealing employee files, wallets, or sensitive mail that is sent to your home, like credit card offers.

3) To detect identity theft, check your credit card bills for unusual activity and review your credit report for suspicious information.

4) If you have been a victim of identity theft, contact your bank, credit card companies, and the Federal Trade Commission. Close any fraudulent accounts set up in your name.

5) Live a precautionary lifestyle by questioning the authenticity of phone callers and e-mail attachments. Ask the post office or a friend to hold your mail while you're on vacation.

CHAPTER 10—MOTIVATION:
Street S.M.A.R.T.s

"Behold the turtle. He makes progress only when he sticks his neck out."

—James Bryant Conant

The Core Curriculum

In school, there are subjects that are part of the core curriculum. English, algebra, biology, history, and physical education are mandatory courses everyone must take sometime during their schooling tenure. Some courses and traits are mandatory for success in the world after graduation, but the fascinating part is that nobody bothers to teach them to you. (People think you will somehow learn them through the process of osmosis.) Instead, you're thrown into the jaws of reality, and although you may have some of these traits from birth, chances are you never sat down to analyze them.

A successful person has many qualities, and if you want to learn about all of them, you can go to your local library or bookstore and head straight for the motivational department. The most fundamental traits you need to succeed (sorry, no carjacking), are outlined on the following pages. In order to be successful throughout life, you need street S.M.A.R.Ts.

In this chapter, you will learn how to:

- use Self-confidence to boost your morale

- create Milestones and goals in your life

- refine your Attitude to a positive one

- make Relaxation an important part of your routine

- use Time management skills effectively

I. Self-Confidence

The Game of Life

Milton wanted to be a scientist, and in 1854 invested all his savings in his education when he enrolled in the Lawrence Scientific School of Cambridge. After only two years of schooling, his parents moved to another city, and being unable to afford to live on his own, Milton was forced to drop out of school and find work in his new home of Hartford, Connecticut. Working as a draftsman for a local locomotive company, he dreamed of one day being a lithographer and owning his own press.

One day, Milton heard of a press that was for sale in Providence, Rhode Island. He traveled to Rhode Island, learned how to use the press, and then bought it. The first big project that came his way was the Republican National Convention in 1860. They asked Milton to produce hundreds of photos of their candidate, Abraham Lincoln. The idea sounded like a good one at the time—until Abraham Lincoln became president. Once elected, the president grew a beard, and no longer resembled his picture from before the election, when he was clean-shaven. All of Milton's pictures were of a clean-shaven Lincoln, and all of Milton's pictures were worthless. Nobody bought them, and with the Civil War just beginning, economic conditions were even worse. Milton had stuck out, yet again.

Then someone brought Milton a board game called "The Checkered Game of Life," and suggested he print mass copies to be sold. Milton still believed in his business and printed 45,000 copies of the game. Luckily, this time he struck gold. People from all over the country bought the game and by 1868, *Milton Bradley* was the foremost manufacturer of board games in the country.

Milton Bradley had confidence in himself. He had suffered setbacks throughout his life. Nonetheless, he didn't let that stand in his way of taking more chances and venturing forth. He knew he had self-worth and value, and therefore continued doing what he was committed to in life. Having self-confidence is the key to winning the real game of life.

The Building Blocks

Having self-confidence in yourself is one of the biggest challenges, yet it is also one of the most important facets of achieving success.

Virtually anything you set out to do will require a confident self-image. Here are a few tips—the building blocks—to help you achieve the proper self-confidence you deserve:

1. **The Rear View Mirror Theory**—Looking back in time is one of the most beneficial ways to improve your confidence. Any time you doubt yourself, think about a similar time when you were faced with a situation that was comparable to the current one. That's what Comic-Cassidy did when he couldn't get a laugh out of people. He remembered when he was only 3, he ran through the streets buck naked and everyone laughed. So he tried it again—and it worked.

2. **The Failing Grade**—The only time you fail is when you let yourself. Thomas Edison, the famous inventor of the light bulb, created over 1,200 imperfect light bulbs before getting it right. He is noted as saying, "I have not failed. Rather, I have created 1,200 bulbs that do not work." Anytime you think you're taking a step back because you were unsuccessful, think of it as an opportunity to learn from your mistakes and improve for the next time. You'll be surprised how much light you will shed on the subject.

3. **Walking Tall**—Your posture makes a huge difference in your self-confidence. Stand tall, walk with pride, and you'll be on your way to having great self-esteem. People will notice you as soon as you walk into a room, realizing you carry yourself with confidence and self-worth. Someone who was extraordinarily short took some advice a little too far and bought a pair of stilts so he could "walk tall." It worked—until he fell, broke his legs from every angle, and had them amputated. So, unless you're employed by the circus, don't use stilts—you'll just end up looking like a clown.

4. **You're Surrounded**—Hang out with people who make you feel important and special. Family, friends, teachers, and counselors who are interested in your personal growth are the people you want to be around. Having a group of people around you who are supportive, funny, and appreciative will boost your self-confidence. For some reason, when the cops,

SWAT teams, and FBI agents surround bank robbers, they don't feel that same love. It's probably those ugly pantyhose they wear over their faces. Think about it, would you want to be friends with someone who put their head in someone's underwear?

5. **Bite-Sized**—Here's an easy and great way to build self-confidence when the task seems overwhelming. Instead of tackling an entire task in one shot, break it down into smaller and more reasonable bites. Doing so will help you feel more comfortable and successful when you accomplish each little goal. As the motivational saying goes, "The only way to eat an elephant is one bite at a time." The only trouble you might encounter is cutting it into bite-sized pieces. For that reason, instead of using the old-fashioned fork and knife, be adventurous and use a chainsaw and pitchfork.

Twinkle, Twinkle, Little Star

Did you ever take an astronomy course, examining the stars in the sky? From a vast distance, they appear small. Look at the sky on a clear night, and you'll see hundreds—no, thousands—of stars. They all look small and relatively similar. Some sparkle a tad bit more, but overall, they're all tiny, far away specs. Now, imagine you are an astronaut traveling into space. As you travel in your spaceship, you're getting closer to one of the thousands of stars you saw from Earth below. This star is gigantic! It's enormous in size, with special colors, unique features, and a glowing radiance.

Most people have a problem with their self-confidence because they don't see themselves as someone who is important or valuable. If you consider yourself invaluable and worthless, chances are you are looking at yourself from very far away—just like a star. You need to take a closer look at who you are and what you have inside. Soon enough, you'll realize that you have an enormous amount of potential and radiance just waiting to be revealed. If you twinkle, twinkle on your little star, you'll never have to wonder where you are.

Worth Every Cent

Jean knew how to capture the audience. She stood in front of hundreds of people, whipping out a $20 bill. She lifted it for everyone to see, and asked, "Is there anyone here who would like this $20?"

Naturally, every hand in the room went up in earnest. People looked at one another with dazed expressions, knowing everyone would want the money. Jean then crumpled it in her hand, crushing it into a little ball. She repeated again, "How many of you still want this $20? Still thinking Jean was crazy, the entire room, full of people, raised their hands once again. Jean then threw the money on the ground and stamped her foot on it, grinding it into the ground. Lifting the mangled money from the floor, she said, "I assume most of you still want this money, right?"

Greeted with many nods, Jean continued, "The $20 bill is how each and every one of us should view ourselves. Every day, people make insulting comments and often do derogatory things to make us feel worthless. But, if you realize that you retain your value no matter what you encounter, your self-confidence will skyrocket."

In life, few people will hesitate to crush, mangle, or trample another person. It happens at school, home, and work. We have to realize we are valuable and have an intrinsic importance that cannot be taken from us—unless we let it be taken. Regardless of what others say or do, we are like a $20 bill—we will always be worth every cent.

The Wrong Crowd

Pete was feeling depressed and sad. These feelings continued for over three months, so he finally decided to go to a psychiatrist and get some professional help. Pete made an appointment, laid down on the couch, and poured his heart out to the doctor sitting beside him. Pete wasn't the type to reveal all his problems to a stranger, but he hoped the doctor would be able to share some words of insight with him.

The psychiatrist asked Pete a few questions, scribbled some notes as Pete talked, then sat in silence, rubbing his chin in confusion. The psychiatrist stared at an eagerly waiting Pete and said with a radiant expression, "I think your problem is low self-esteem. It is very common among losers."

Poor Pete didn't get the answer he was looking for. Nobody wants to hear from another person—especially one they're paying—that they are a loser. Human beings are delicate, and need to hear positive reinforcement when they are down. It's for that reason it is especially important to hang out with the right crowd, as discussed above. If you associate with people who aid you in your journey to self-confidence, the only loser will be the person who goes to Pete's psychiatrist.

False Teeth

Having self-confidence is about being honest and true to who you are. There is no need to pretend or fake your personality. Just be true to yourself, and your personality and self-confidence will shine through. Consider the sign one dentist posted on his office door: "Be True to Your Teeth, or They Will Be False to You."

II. Milestones

GOAL!

Goals are what separate winning from losing in soccer. Score more goals than the other team, and your team walks away victorious. Life is similar, although the only competition you have is yourself. Having goals, dreams, and milestones in life is critical. Goals can come on a smaller scale, such as what to accomplish each day, week, or month. Goals also take the shape of long-term dreams, such as acquiring a desired job, having a family, or perfecting your hobby. Regardless of your situation in life, having aspirations and mile-markers for yourself will ultimately determine how many "goals" you score.

The Wright Opportunity

Dr. Samuel Langley was a prestigious professor and served on the board at the Smithsonian Institute. He believed he would be the inventor of modern-day aviation, and would create the airplane. The government believed he could achieve it, and granted him $50,000 to use his textbook knowledge and the research he had been doing for many years on this daunting task.

In the fall of 1903, Dr. Langley attempted this amazing feat with his engineer, Charles Manley. Mr. Manley climbed into what was called the Great Aerodrome, and within seconds of takeoff, the engine fell apart, and the Great Aerodrome didn't look so great anymore. Dr. Langley and his crew were devastated, embarrassed, and humiliated. But that wasn't about to stop them.

Approximately eight weeks after the fiasco, Dr. Langley attempted it again. This time it was even worse, with the pilot almost being killed. The criticism was harsher this time around, as the public was angered and disappointed with the decade-long project. This was too much for Dr. Langley. He gave up his dream and career, leaving all his efforts behind.

Only three months after the second failure, two brothers, Orville and Wilber Wright, took over where Dr. Langley had left off. They believed that aviation could become a reality and took their stab at it on December 17, 1903. To the world's shock, they flew the very first airplane, leaving Dr. Langley in the dust.

Creating goals is easy. Seeing them through adversity to fruition is a whole other ballgame. To be successful at what you set out to achieve, you have to be willing to fail—maybe even with public humiliation—numerous times. Learn to use those errors and mistakes to help build your skill into one where you can accomplish the goal. Dr. Langley ultimately failed because he quit after the second failed attempt. If he had moved forward and learned from his mistakes, chances are he—and not the *Wright Brothers*—would be the inventor of the airplane. Be optimistic and realistic when establishing goals, realizing that anything that doesn't achieve the results you hope for is only a steppingstone. You have to be willing to fail if you ultimately want to succeed—and once you do, you'll be soaring much higher than you ever imagined.

How to Make the Score
Setting goals can be intimidating, and if not done properly, can have a reverse effect if you're not careful. Use these helpful tips when outlining your goals and ambitions:

1. **Dead-On Target**—Get as specific as possible when making a goal. You can't be wishy-washy or unsure. Determine exactly what you want before moving on to any of the next steps. Having a defined goal will set the tone for how you set off on your journey to achieve it. So be dead-on target and you'll end up with a bull's-eye.

2. **No Pain, No Gain**—Sometimes you have to challenge yourself. Be sure your goals are specific and challenging. Push yourself, within reasonable limitations, because if there's no pain, there's usually very little—or no—gain. Jumping out of an airplane without a parachute or lying on a railroad track as a train approaches might seem like a good way to challenge yourself, but those rails are freezing cold. You could die from hypothermia!

3. **The Real Deal**—While pushing yourself to run the extra mile, be sure your goal is realistic in nature. People often set unrealistic goals, and when they don't achieve them, the result is disappointment and despair. Five-year-old Fred was the most recent victim of a motivational seminar. The instructors brainwashed those kids into thinking they could really do *anything* if they set their mind to it. Fred loved Superman,

and convinced himself he, too, was from planet Krypton. Poor Fred remembered he could do anything if he set his mind to it, and when he leaped off the teacher's very tall desk, he flapped his arms frantically, trying to fly. Fred was right—he did fly—right into the emergency room for breaking every bone in his body. In honor of Fred, change the cliché to, "You can do *almost* anything if you set your mind to it."

4. **Time Line**—Having a specified amount of time to accomplish a goal will help you track your progress. If you give yourself two weeks to complete a research paper, you will feel the urgent and pressing need to finish it within that time frame. If you leave it open-ended, do you honestly believe you'll make time to do it? Of course, for those of you who are study-a-holics, spend all your free time writing scientific proposals for professional journals, and go to sleep at 7:30 p.m., you can disregard all of the aforementioned advice.

5. **Put It in Writing**—Goals work much better once they are on paper. It might seem corny or childish, but the biggest babies are the ones who ignore this advice. Write down the goals you set, the challenges you anticipate, the realistic expectations you have, and the time period in which you believe you can accomplish them. Put it in writing, and your success won't be erased.

Killer Instinct

For Todd's science fair project, he decided to try something different. Instead of exploding volcanoes or solar electricity pads, Todd bought a mini-shark, and placed it in a tank with a tiny goldfish. Todd placed a clear glass divider in the middle of the tank, separating the shark from the goldfish. The shark naturally made a lunge for the goldfish after only minutes, but instead of feasting, he took a beating. Todd purposely didn't feed the shark, making him hungrier with each passing moment. He fed the goldfish every day, making sure it was nourished and well-fed. Seeing the goldfish with hungry eyes, the shark continued to slam into the glass divider, time after time.

Several weeks later, the shark finally stopped slamming into the glass partition, and instead just swam in circles. The shark was bruised and tired of getting beaten, so he stopped trying. Todd then did the unthinkable. He removed the glass partition, and waited to see if the shark would lunge at the helpless goldfish. Incredibly, the shark didn't even attempt to cross the line where the glass partition had been. The goldfish he continued to feed daily, while the shark was starved. After a little more time, the shark died from starvation, while the goldfish lived a risk-free life.

In life, we often muster up the energy and drive, like the shark, and go after what we want. We set goals and have the drive to lunge forward, only to slam into a glass wall. We get hit time after time, getting bruised and hurt. Sometimes, we give up from discouragement and disappointment, swimming in our little circles on "our side" of the glass. The lesson Todd learned from his experiment was that no matter what the circumstances, if you are starving for something, go after it, no matter how many times you hit the glass wall. Keep hitting it and one day, you might be surprised to find it's been lifted for you. And even if it hasn't, keep slamming into it and you might break it down. Once you establish your goals, and are starving to satisfy them, use your killer instinct and never give up on achieving them.

III. Attitude

Pop, Goes the Weasel

Frank Epperson was a happy-go-lucky eleven-year-old. In the winter of 1905, Frank mixed the powder from a soda pop mix with water, hoping to make soda for himself. After accidentally leaving it outside overnight, Frank returned in the morning to find his mixture completely frozen. In the middle of the frozen concoction was the mixing stick he had used to stir the powder and water.

Instead of being upset, aggravated, or frustrated, Frank pulled up the frozen mix by the stick and decided to take a lick. Little did he know he was on to something big. He called it the Epperson Icicle, and during the next summer, he made them in bulk and sold them in the local neighborhood for five cents each. He would later rename his invention the *Popsicle*, as it initially contained soda pop.

Frank Epperson is the perfect example of someone who had a great attitude, even when something didn't go as he had planned. He attempted to make soda, and instead, his treat was frozen. He could have thrown it away or become irate over the situation. Instead, because of his positive attitude, he transformed the situation into a famous frozen treat found in all major grocery stores. Having a good attitude in life assures that nobody will ever be able to pop your bubble.

Lock and Key

Having a positive and upbeat attitude in life is as important as it comes. When you venture into the working world, nothing beats a positive attitude. Good grades, great internships, and connections will unlock the door of any Fortune 500 company. But, once you get past the gatekeepers, the one key that will determine your success or failure is your attitude. Being positive, happy, and upbeat—even when you don't want to be—is the key to success. How you develop your attitude will ultimately determine how easily you unlock your dreams.

Sign Language

Don't believe the importance of attitude? That's okay, don't take anyone's word for it. Take a look at the numeric value of certain words, and you'll see this isn't made up from thin air. In fact, there are signs in the language we speak. The alphabet has a numeric code system. Each letter represents a number in ascending order. For example, A is 1, B is 2, C is 3, etc. The entire alphabet, in numeric value is:

A B C D E F G H I J K L M N O P Q R S T U V W X Y Z
1 2 3 4 5 6 7 8 9 10 11 12 13 14 15 16 17 18 19 20 21 22 23 24 25 26

Considering the numeric system, take a moment to study the following words:

K N O W L E D G E
11 +14+ 15 +23+ 12+ 5 + 4+ 7 + 5 = 96

H A R D W O R K
8+ 1 +18+ 4 +23 + 15+ 18 + 11 = 98

A T T I T U D E
1 +20+20+9+20+ 21 +4 + 5 = 100

Nobody will tell you that knowledge and hard work are useless. They're important, and essential to getting into college and landing your first job. But keep in mind that the information you learn and the late nights you spend in the library won't help unless you coat them with a positive attitude. Be optimistic, encouraging, and upbeat, and you'll be amazed at how much extra credit you'll receive.

Tuning the 'Tude

Acquiring and maintaining a positive attitude isn't easy. But a few simple tools will help keep you on track:

1. **Expect the Unexpected**—Life isn't easy, but sometimes we expect it to be. When you realize that life throws you curve balls, and things aren't always as cookie-cutter perfect as we would like them to be, you won't expect a smooth ride without any waves. Expect the unexpected obstacles that float your way. So, if it normally takes you 20 minutes to drive to school, give yourself 30. Why? Because there will always be something you don't expect to happen, such as an accident, poor weather conditions, or aliens abducting innocent civilians (in

which case, it might take longer than 30 minutes).

2. **What's the Worst That Could Happen?**—Quite frankly, not much. This is a question too often overlooked. Anytime you feel your positive attitude melting, ask yourself if it's really that bad. Sometimes it is—in which case you should dial 911—but the majority of the time it isn't. Human nature gives us a tendency to inflate our problems with hot air—and lift us high above reality. So keep life in perspective, and your positive attitude will be airtight. If you truly don't think every day is a good day, just try missing one. (Legal Note: Not recommended.)

3. **The Critical Factor**—Many people start off with great attitudes, but lose them very quickly when they are criticized by others. They lose faith in themselves, and quickly shed the optimism they started with. Look at constructive criticism as a factor that will help you grow and develop. Anytime someone criticizes you, look at it as a way to improve and move closer toward achieving a goal. Here's an example: The next time someone says, "You are a worthless, piece-of-garbage, obnoxious, arrogant, loathsome, and empty person," simply respond, "Thanks, I'll try to improve on that."

4. **Go Shopping!**—Okay, maybe this isn't for everyone, but it's the concept (and not the example, so calm down, stingy parents) that's being emphasized. Sometimes, the best way to acquire a positive attitude is to do something you genuinely enjoy. Go to the movies, call a friend, roller blade on the beach, or, if all else fails, go shopping! Whatever the activity, take a proactive approach to putting yourself in a good mood—and you'll be shocked to see how cheaply happiness comes.

5. **From the Outside In**—Believe it or not, pretending to act happy often puts you in a genuinely good mood. A smile is a curved line that sets many things straight. Make your attitude one of them. As hard as it may be, force yourself to smile and act with enthusiasm. Stand tall and proud, and before you know it, you'll feel good about yourself and your attitude.

A Grand Lesson

Little Timothy was having problems with his attitude. At only 10 years of age, he believed that everyone at school hated him and thought he was a pain to be around. His teacher, Rex, knew otherwise. Rex took Timothy to the Grand Canyon, and made him stand on the very edge of that spectacular scene. He asked Timothy to yell at the top of his lungs, "You're a loser!" Obeying his teacher, Timothy screamed, "You're a loser!" Echoing back several times, the phrase "You're a loser!" faded just a little each time.

Rex then told Timothy to scream, "You're the greatest!" Following his teacher's instructions, Timothy screamed the words. Once again, the reverberation of his own voice shouting, "You're the greatest!" lingered in the distance. Rex then told Timothy that this is how the world operates. Whatever you put out into the world will be thrown right back at you. The boomerang effect is real: inject a positive attitude into society, and society will show you a very positive reaction. Just realize that most attitudes are contagious. So is yours worth catching?

IV. Relaxation

Fooling Around on the Job

During the 1870s, Walter Morrison worked for a pie company in Connecticut. When work was finished and people were unwinding toward the end of the day, there was a pass time for the coworkers to throw around empty pie tins, which had the company name on them.

In the 1950s Walter had quit working for the pie company, and instead, invented a metal throwing toy for kids to play with. He quickly got word that metal was too dangerous for children, so he changed it to plastic. He called it the "Flying Saucer" at first, but after changing the material from metal to plastic, he decided to give the toy a new name. He recalled his younger days when he and his friends would throw around the empty pie tins. The name of the pie company was the Frisbie Pie Company, with the name Frisbie stamped on the pie tins. Walter decided to name his toy the *Frisbee*.

The workers at the Frisbie Pie Company knew it was important to let loose occasionally. They understood that people couldn't work all the time. There needed to be some outlet to relax and loosen up. Life has changed drastically since the 1870s, but the one aspect that remains true is that people need to take breaks and other measures to relax.

Chill Out

Relaxing is an aspect of life some people need to improve upon, while others have mastered it as a fine art—and in some cases, they've mastered it too well. Being able to relax has multiple components to it, with a steady balance being the ideal scenario. Being a workaholic is not conducive to any aspect of life, except one—work. And even then, it is questionable. On the other hand, an overabundance of loosening up can be a sign of laziness and lack of motivation. It is therefore crucial to find the happy medium in between, knowing when to work hard—and when to chill out.

A Pain in the Neck

How do you know if you're stressed out and need to relax? Although this list is not complete, the main signs should raise a red flag. Here are some of the signs that you are overextending yourself:

- Falling asleep is becoming consistently difficult
- Concentrating during the day is a struggle
- It's hard to focus on one issue at a time
- You are worried, anxious, or sad for no apparent reason
- Muscles in your body ache, such as your back and neck, or you have an upset stomach (and you didn't fall off your motorcycle the day before)

How Can I Get Rid of Stress?

The first thing you need to evaluate is whether the problem is one you can fix through simple relaxation techniques, or if you require medical attention. Try some of the relaxation and stress-relieving techniques below, and if they do not work, see a doctor or a therapist who can custom-tailor your treatment.

Ways to De-Stress

Most of these techniques are psychological exercises to help you escape the pressures and stresses of daily life. They don't work for everyone but many people have used them and benefited greatly. Give them a try and, who knows, you might feel more relaxed because of them.

1. **Take a Deep Breath**—And hold it for about ten seconds. Exhale slowly and deeply, believing that you are escaping the harsh reality of life for those few seconds. This can be especially helpful during a final exam or intense research project. However, a warning for the daredevils among you: If you enjoy holding your breath too long, depriving your brain of oxygen, turning beet red, and passing out, call an ambulance immediately. Maybe you'd better call the ambulance *before* you fall unconscious.

2. **Take a Break**—Not all of us have this luxury, but more often than not, you can take a break from what you're working on. If it's an intense term paper you are researching and you find yourself stressed out, take an hour and go watch some TV. Read that novel you've been itching to finish. Heck, you can even jump in the shower for thirty minutes. Whatever relaxes you, do it for a short time. Limit how long your break will be, but when you're on a break, be on a break. Don't think about

work or the stress. Just unwind and use that positive energy to finish the project when you return.

3. **Do Some Short Physical Exercises**—This one works really well. If you feel lethargic and tired during the day, stand up and do some jumping jacks. It might feel strange, difficult, or weird at first, but a short physical exercise break will get your blood moving and give you a boost of energy to finish the day. Nonetheless, this tactic doesn't work well on the first day of work. Your boss, Milton, might get a bit concerned if he catches you using your mouse cable as a jump rope. But, if you can't resist the urge to use your tiny cubicle as a personal gym, take a shower afterward.

4. **Go on a Mental Vacation**—Go to a quiet room, a place where you will not be disturbed and where you feel comfortable. Sit in a comfortable chair or lie down on a sofa or bed, and imagine a place you would really like to be. Close your eyes and take a step into this different world. It can be a pool, the beach, somewhere in the Caribbean, or skiing in a beautiful resort in Colorado. Whatever you imagine, think about the details of where you are—the temperature, how it smells, feels, tastes, and looks. WARNING: Be careful. If you do this *too* well, you might fall asleep and the whole purpose of your relaxation technique will be lost! Where do you think you are—on vacation?!

5. **Massage Therapy**—Contrary to popular belief, the rich and famous aren't the only ones who get massages. You don't have to go to a fancy spa in Beverly Hills to reap the benefits of such activities. There are many books, Web sites, and articles written on how to give yourself a massage. No, you didn't misread that—you can give yourself a massage. There are medically proven pressure points in the hands and feet that, when rubbed in a certain manner, can relieve a tremendous amount of stress and anxiety. It can be fun, cheap, and most importantly—effective. Just be careful not to get caught up in childhood memories. Because if you start chanting, "This little piggy went to the market, this little piggy went home...," your roommate will make sure your little piggy finds a new home.

Bird Watching

King George was on a mission. He wanted to find a portrait that epitomized peace. He proposed a contest for the entire village, with the winner receiving a big monetary reward. With many paintings entered in the contest, the king finally selected two that were his favorites. The first was of a serene lake, with a clear blue sky hovering above. The second picture was a painting of rugged mountains with heavy rain pouring down on them. A streak of lightning brightened this painting, striking down on the mountains below. In the corner of this second painting, a bird had established a nest for her young. The mother bird was sitting with her young, holding them close to her.

King George looked from one painting to the other, wondering which one truly captured the image of peace. Finally, King George declared the second painting the winner. He explained, "Peace doesn't mean you are in a place where there is no commotion, danger, or stress. Real peace means when you are in the trenches of demanding exterior factors, yet inside your heart, you feel calm and serene—like the mother bird with her young. That is why the second painting will win the prize for portraying peace."

Being able to relax and be at peace is truly in our head. Some think the most relaxing lifestyle would be when they had made millions of dollars and could lounge by the pool, sipping a piña colada. Yet we can have the most relaxing life in the world no matter what we do—if we let ourselves. Exterior factors will always be in our life. Our job is to use breaks, vacations, visual imagery, and physical release to relax our muscles and mind. If we can learn to use these techniques effectively, we won't need millions of dollars to feel rested—because we'll already feel like a million bucks.

V. Time Management

Gambling Problem

During the eighteenth century, people acted, spoke, and dressed differently from today. John Montagu, an English earl, had one addiction that has survived until this very day: gambling. He refused to leave the gaming tables for any reason. He delayed going to the bathroom, became sleep deprived, and even stopped going to the royal dining room for meals. One day, he came up with an idea of how he wouldn't have to sacrifice his beloved card games for his hunger. He requested that he be served sliced meats and cheese in between two pieces of bread. He would snack on this delicacy, and after doing this for many years, became well known throughout the land. John Montagu was England's 4th Earl of Sandwich, and as a result, the name *sandwich* has been associated with the meal he ate.

John Montagu didn't believe in wasting time. He had a desire to gamble, and would stop at nothing to achieve it. While his motivations were questionable, his concept of time management was perfect. He maximized his time while not starving in the process. Time management can be crucial in your ability to perform multiple tasks. And, as life becomes increasingly difficult with school, family, friends, and work, time management is a skill you can't afford to gamble away.

A Science Experiment With Fred

Fred the science teacher came into a class ready to perform an experiment. Fred took an empty jar and filled it with big rocks until no more could fit inside. He then poured a bag of gravel into the jar, which filled all the space in between the big rocks. Fred then opened a bag of sand, pouring that into the jar as well. Naturally, the sand filled the empty spaces where the gravel and large rocks did not. Finally, when the class thought the jar was at its maximum capacity, Fred poured a glass of water into the jar, the liquid quickly spread throughout the jar. He capped the jar with a lid, screwing it on tight.

Fred explained that this experiment was the nature of time management. Each day, we have tasks that are like rocks—they're big, bulky, and consume the majority of our time. Nonetheless, we need to fill in the "empty spaces" with gravel—smaller tasks that can be squeezed into the smaller time slots. Then we need to micromanage our time even further, squeezing the intangible sand in there. After that comes the daily issues that are all over the place—just like the water. Our job is to fit all of these tasks and jobs under the lid of one jar. If we can find a way to squeeze them all in, then we'll be in great shape. The trick is to fit them in without overflowing the jar—and making a big mess.

So How Do I Manage My Time?

Well, the answer is simple. Plan, plan, plan! If you can plan properly, you'll never have a problem with time management. Some people think that planning is a waste of time. Nothing could be farther from the truth. Planning is like the foundation of a high-rise building. If you have a rock-solid foundation, everything on top will be sturdier. Effective planning means you map out a strategy for the tasks you need to accomplish, prioritize them, and then designate a certain amount of time for each.

1. **Decide What Needs to Be Done:** Write down on a piece of paper all the tasks you need to accomplish: homework, phone calls, plucking your nose hairs, bank robbing, getting your tattoo polished, and any other jobs you need to complete. Make sure the list is a reasonable one. These should be activities you expect to honestly finish in one day or evening. If you aren't careful with this first step, you'll be setting yourself up for disappointment—and disaster.

2. **Prioritize:** Now that you've outlined exactly what you need to accomplish, go up and down the list, giving each item a priority number. The first item should be the most important, one that has urgency attached to it. Activities with deadlines customarily fly to the top of the list. Give priority to the important things in life, like watering your pet rock and pampering your poisonous snake Slither with lots of love. (For those who own pet rocks with stunted growth: sunlight helps bring out their true growth potential.)

3. **Prime Time:** The next crucial step is to write down an estimated length of time for the activity. Budgeting your time is a great exercise in guessing how long each activity will take. Be honest, use reason, and calculate accordingly—because

now you have to execute your plan. If some of these tasks are your daily routines, you probably have a good feel for how long they should take. For example, watering the pet rock may only take 5 minutes, while playtime with Slither can range from 30-40 minutes, depending on how tightly he's wrapped around your neck.

4. **Stick to the Plan:** Once the plan is under way, it will be easy to get sidetracked and distracted with other things. Phone calls, e-mails, news reports, IM's, and your mom asking you to take out the garbage can be monkey wrenches in your plan. Even if you have to attend to something small in between, get back on course. Keeping the bigger picture in mind is ultimately the most important aspect of time management. Completing the example from above, don't get too wound up in playing with Slither, and slowly lose sight of the big picture—like living to see the next day.

Send Me a Postcard

Have you ever noticed the way you write a postcard? When you're on vacation and lounging around the campfire, you decide it would be nice to send your friend a card telling her about your vacation. You usually start writing with normal-sized letters, taking up a lot of space. Before you know it, you're cramming in a lot of other information you wanted to say, but now realize you simply don't have room for it. So you start to write smaller. And smaller. And then you write so small that your hand hurts. Soon enough, only someone with a magnifying glass could read what you've written! The worst part is that when it's all over, you didn't even write about the best part of your vacation!

The same is true with the use of your time every day. You probably begin your day with activities that take up a lot of time— sleep, coffee, and grogginess—and figure you'll get to the important things later on. Then it's suddenly time for lunch, and by this time, you might have accomplished some of the things you wanted to do, but figure you have the whole afternoon to take care of the more important issues. After lunch, you're hit with the sluggish afternoon slump, and by the time night rolls around, you find yourself writing smaller and smaller, trying to cram everything important into the day. By the time you go to sleep, it's quite common that you will not have accomplished some of the items you felt were most significant. Consider your day like a postcard—write in a reasonable font, and say the most important things first. Doing so will prevent you from squinting—and using a magnifying glass.

Eenie, Meenie, Miny, Moe

Judy was a hardworking woman, who was approached by a man conducting a survey. The man asked her several questions relating to what she did for a living, where she grew up, and how many people she had in her family.

"My husband and I have four kids," Judy replied.

"Oh really? What are their names?" asked the man.

"Eenie, Meenie, Miny, and George," Judy said.

The surveyor raised his eyebrows in curiosity, wondering why Judy and her husband changed the pattern they were headed toward. "George? Why George?" asked the man.

"Because we didn't want any Moe," she quipped.

As corny as it might be, Judy and her husband had a plan—even if it wasn't a foolproof one. They knew that after the fourth child, they did not want to have any more, so they named him accordingly. Time management is applicable to every area of life—school, work, extracurricular activities, or simply hobbies you enjoy. You need to have a plan of action, know how important each one is, and then decide how much time to allot. Having a plan from the beginning will ultimately determine whether all of your desired goals are met.

Chapter 10 Homework Reading–Recommended Books

Title: *Ultimate Secrets of Total Self-Confidence*
Author: Robert Anthony
ISBN: 0425101703
Publisher: Penguin Group

Title: *One Minute Manager*
Authors: Kenneth H. Blanchard, Spencer Johnson, Ken Blanchard
ISBN: 0060567503
Publisher: HarperCollins Publishers

Title: *Success Through a Positive Mental Attitude*
Authors: Napoleon Hill, W. Clement Stone
ISBN: 0671743228
Publisher: Simon & Schuster Adult Publishing Group

Title: *Time Management from the Inside Out: The Foolproof Plan
for Taking Control of Your Schedule and Your Life*
Author: Julie Morgenstern
ISBN: 0805075909
Publisher: Henry Holt & Company, Incorporated

Title: *Getting Things Done: The Art of Stress-Free Productivity*
Author: David Allen
ISBN: 0142000280
Publisher: Penguin Group

Chapter 10 Summary—The Least You Need to Know in Order to Pass the Class

1) Improve your self-confidence by looking at similar circumstances in your past, using failures as lessons for the future, walking tall with good posture, and hanging around the right people.

2) Set goals for yourself by being specific, and by making them challenging, time-coding them, and writing them down on paper.

3) Maintain a positive attitude, keep life in perspective, expect the unexpected, and look at criticism as a constructive way to improve.

4) Take daily relaxation breaks by going on mental vacations, doing physical exercise, and taking deep breaths.

5) Effective time management skills develop when you plan, prioritize, allot sufficient time for each activity, and see your plan through to the end without getting sidetracked.

Appendix A: Apartment, House, and Moving Resource Guide

APARTMENTS & HOUSES

Apartments.com
Phone: 312-601-5000
www.apartments.com

Rent.com
310-581-2774
www.rent.com

RentNet.com
Phone: 805-557-2300
Fax: 805-557-2680
www.RentNet.com

ForRent.com
Phone: 1-888-539-1150
www.ForRent.com

Apartment Guide
Fax: 770-729-2632
www.apartmentguide.com

Rent Wave
Phone: 1-800-710-LIST (5478)
Fax: 310-581-2033
www.RentWave.com

Off Campus Network
908-534-3287
www.offcampusnetwork.com

Homes.com
1-888-329-7576
www.homes.com

American Home Guides
www.americanhomeguides.com

New Home Guide
www.newhomeguide.com

MOVING

U-Haul
1-800-468-4285
www.uhaul.com

Mayflower Transit
636-305-4000
www.mayflower.com

Budget Moving
Budget Rent A Car System, Inc.
1-800-527-0700
www.budget.com

ABF U-Pack
1-800-355-1696
www.upack.com

Moving U
1-877-MOVING-U
www.moving.com

Monster Moving
www.monstermoving.com

Delta Van Lines
1-800-544-1380
www.deltavanlines.com

PODS
1-888-776-PODS
www.pods.com

Door-to-Door Moving and Storage
1-888-505-3667
www.doortodoor.com

Marlin Van Lines
1-888-627-5460
www.marlinvanlines.com

Allied Van Lines
1-800-823-0755
www.alliedvan.com

Viking Van Lines
1-866-984-5464
www.vikingvanlines.com

Appendix B: Car Resource Guide

FOR MSRP, INVOICE PRICES, CAR QUOTES, & REBATES:

Dealix Corporation
Phone: 650-599-5500
Fax: 650-599-5501
www.invoicedealers.com

Edmunds
Phone: 310-309-6300
www.edmunds.com

Autoweb
General information: 949-225-4500
Autoweb Customers: 1-877-381-7433
www.autoweb.com

Car.com
Phone: 1-800-CAR-COM-0 (1-800-227-2660)
Fax: 248-269-7300
www.car.com

Autonation
Phone: 1-800-859-6442
www.autonation.com

CarsDirect.com
Phone: 1-800-431-2500
www.carsdirect.com

Autobytel, Incs.
Phone: 1-888-422-8999 EXT. 3050
ConsumerCare@autobytel.com
www.autobytel.com

Stone Age
Phone: 1-800-STONEAGE
Fax: 248-269-7300
www.stoneage.com

FOR LEASES:

Lease Compare
Phone: 513-527-7700
Fax: 513-527-7705
www.leasecompare.com

Prime Lease
Phone: 954-321-6099
www.primelease.com

LeaseGuide.com
www.leaseguide.com

ONLINE AUCTION CARS:

eBay Inc.
www.ebaymotors.com

USED PRICES OF CARS:

NADAguides.com
www.NADAguides.com

Kelley Blue Book
Phone: 1-800-BLUE-BOOK. Choose menu option 4 and then 1.
www.kbb.com

Edmunds
Phone: 310-309-6300
www.edmunds.com

Cars.com
Phone: 312-601-5616
www.cars.com

VEHICLE BACKGROUND HISTORY & INFO REPORTS (FOR USED CARS):

CarFax
Phone: 703-934-2664
Fax: 703-218-2465
www.carfax.com

Auto Check
www.autocheck.com

TO GET CONSUMER REPORTS ON CARS (FOR NEW CARS):

Car and Driver
Phone: 734-971-3600
www.CarAndDriver.com

Car Review (Consumer Review)
Phone: 650-212-8600
www.CarReview.com

TO GET YOUR CREDIT REPORT & CREDIT SCORE:

Equifax
Phone: 1-800-685-1111
www.equifax.com

Experian
Phone: 1-800-888-4213
www.experian.com

Transunion
Phone: 1-888-397-3742
www.transunion.com

True Credit
www.truecredit.com

TO GET AN AUTO LOAN:

E-Loan
Phone: 925-847-6200
Fax: 925-847-0831
www.eloan.com

LendingTree Inc.
Phone: 1-800-555-TREE
www.lendingtree.com

Capital One Auto Finance
Phone: 1-800-689-1789 & 619-232-5660
Fax: 1-888-412-7543
www.capitaloneautofinance.com

EXTENDED WARRANTIES:

Warranty Direct
Phone: 1-800-632-4222
www.warrantydirect.com

1SourceAutoWarranty.com
Phone: 1-888-905-5700
Fax: 303-741-2813
www.1sourceautowarranty.com

AUTO INSURANCE:

AAA
Phone: 1-800-924-6141
www.AAA.com

Geico
Phone: 1-877-206-0215
www.geico.com

State Farm Insurance
Phone: 1-877-SF4-BANK (1-877-734-2265).
www.statefarm.com

The Progressive Corporation
Phone: 1-800-PROGRESSIVE (1-800-776-4737)
www.progressive.com

Insurance.com
Phone: 1-866-533-0227
www.insurance.com

21st Century Insurance
Phone: 818-704-3700
www.21st.com

Insure Me
Phone: 1-800-INSURE-ME (1-800-467-8736).
Fax: 303-741-6670
www.insureme.com

Appendix C: Money Resource Guide

BANKS

Washington Mutual
1-800-788-7000
www.wamu.com

Bank of America
1-800-622-8731
www.bankofamerica.com

Am Trust
1-888-696-4444
www.amtrust.com

US Bank
1-800-US-Banks
www.usbank.com

SunTrust
1-800-279-4824
www.suntrust.com

CitiBank
1-800-627-3999
www.citibank.com

Chase Manhattan
1-800-Chase-24
www.chase.com

Wells Fargo Bank
1-800-869-3557
www.wellsfargo.com

Wachovia
1-800-922-4684
www.wachovia.com

ING
1-888-ING-0727
www.ing.com

BUYING STOCKS

Ameritrade
1-800-454-9272
www.ameritrade.com

Schwab
1-866-855-9102
www.schwab.com

TD Waterhouse
1-800-934-4448
www.tdwaterhouse.com

E*Trade
1-800-387-2331
www.etrade.com

BUYING MUTUAL FUNDS

AIM
1-800-959-4246
www.aimfunds.com

American Funds
1-800-421-4120
www.americanfunds.com

Fidelity
1-800-544-6666
www.fidelity.com

Putnam
1-800-225-1581
www.putnam.com

Vanguard
1-877-662-7447
www.vanguard.com

Oppenheimer
 1-888-470-0862
www.oppenheimerfunds.com

Appendix D: Resource Guide for Nutrition, Health, and Cooking

Health:

Web MD
Phone: 201-703-3400
Fax: 201-703-3401
www.webmd.com

HealthFinder
www.healthfinder.gov

American Medical Association
1-800-621-8335
www.ama-assn.org

Kids Health—Everyday Illness & Injuries
www.kidshealth.org

Nutrition & Fitness:

Food and Nutrition information Center
Phone: 301-504-5719
Fax: 301-504-6409
www.nal.usda.gov/fnic

American Society for Nutritional Sciences
www.nutrition.org

Recipes and Meals:

www.foodtv.com
www.Cooking.com
www.meals.com
www.verybestbaking.com
www.allrecipes.com
www.epicurious.com
www.cooksrecipes.com
www.mealsforyou.com

Index

About the Author

While attending high school in Miami Beach, Craig was a writer for and the editor of the high school publication. At age 18, he coauthored his first book, *Courage to Change,* which was printed and sold locally in Miami. Attending Yeshiva University and the Sy Syms School of Business, he received his Bachelor of Science in Accounting, graduating Summa Cum Laude. In his graduating year, he received the prestigious Mildred Schlessberg Accounting Society Award for outstanding service.

His work experience includes Ramada Plaza Resorts and Mass Mutual Financial Group, where he obtained his life and health insurance license. He is a licensed CPA, and is currently working for the leader of the Big Four international accounting firms.

Currently conducting monthly motivational seminars, Craig has frequently lectured at various institutions in New York City and Los Angeles. He has also addressed college students at over ten campuses, including New York University, Boston University, Rutgers University, and Arizona State University. He resides with his incredible wife, Samantha, in South Florida. He can be contacted through the publisher at CHirsch@WindowViewPublications.com.

Give the Ultimate Gift of Life After School to Recent Graduates, Friends, and Colleagues

CHECK YOUR LOCAL BOOKSTORE OR ORDER HERE

☐ YES! I want __ copies of *School's Out* at $14.95 (12% off the cover price) each, plus $3 shipping and handling per book. Please allow up to ten business days for delivery.

My check or money order for $_____ is enclosed.

Name_____

Organization_____

Address_____

City/State/Zip_____

Phone_____

Email_____

Please make your check payable
to Window View Publications and return to:

Craig Hirsch
c/o Window View Publications
P.O. Box 81-4223
Hollywood, FL 33081-4223

Email: Sales@WindowViewPublications.com

Printed in the United States
114091LV00003B/6/A